THE YEAR
IN TENNIS 2006

DAVIS CUP
by **BNP PARIBAS**

ITF
International Tennis Federation

Text by Chris Bowers

The International Tennis Federation

Universe

First published in the United States of America in 2007 by
UNIVERSE PUBLISHING A Division of Rizzoli International Publications, Inc.
300 Park Avenue South, New York, NY 10010
www.rizzoliusa.com

© 2007 by the International Tennis Federation
140807

2006 2007 2008 / 10 9 8 7 6 5 4 3 2 1

Designed by Domino 4 Limited, Weybridge, United Kingdom
Printed in Italy

ISBN: 0-7893-1547-5
ISBN 13: 978-0-7893-1547-2

CONTENTS

PRESIDENT'S MESSAGE

THE FINAL OF THE 2006 DAVIS CUP BY BNP PARIBAS was the perfect illustration of just how international this great team event is. It also showed that founder Dwight Davis's dream of creating greater understanding between nations through sport is still being met today.

The Argentinian team traveled more than eight thousand miles to Moscow to contest the final against Russia. In five thrilling matches played in the best possible spirit in front of a capacity crowd of 11,500 at the Olympic Stadium, they narrowly lost 3–2 to the hosts.

When Marat Safin clinched the winning point in the fourth-set tiebreak of the decisive fifth rubber against Jose Acasuso, the contrasting scenes on either side of the net were the most eloquent expression of how much it matters to a player to win the Davis Cup. As the Russians invaded the court and hoisted Safin aloft, Acasuso stumbled tearfully to his chair to be consoled by his teammates. But it also spoke volumes that, by the time both the Russian and Argentinian players attended that night's gala dinner, they were both singing cheerfully and chatting with each other in a display of true friendship.

The deciding tie of the 2006 Davis Cup by BNP Paribas featured two teams with enviable strength in depth, the Argentines led by the indomitable David Nalbandian, and the Russian effort being spearheaded by Safin and Dmitry Tursunov. These two nations are still in the process of establishing their legacies in the sport of tennis. Russia, which won its second Davis Cup title but first at home, is slightly ahead of Argentina in this process, but nobody doubts that the South Americans will soon lift the trophy for the first time. I hope that they get over their disappointment very soon, because their time will come.

But the Davis Cup by BNP Paribas is about more than just the final. It remains the largest annual team competition in sports, its international reach being such that Russia and Argentina were two of 133 nations that took part in 2006. The World Group alone, which features the leading sixteen nations, was played across four continents. Other nations competed in one of three regional zones, Europe/Africa, Americas, and Asia/Oceania, where winning promotion and avoiding relegation can be as important as capturing the Davis Cup trophy itself.

Players continue to be irresistibly drawn to the Davis Cup by BNP Paribas. The leading men take part in spite of the demands of the crowded tennis calendar, nineteen of the world's top twenty doing so in 2006. A total of 547 players competed across all zones during the year. As well as giving players a near-unique opportunity in tennis to represent their countries, it often provides their only chance to play in front of a home crowd.

The scale, not the spirit, of the Davis Cup competition is what has changed since it was first played 106 years ago. More than half a million people attended Davis Cup ties in 2006, and it was followed by millions more fans on television and via the Internet, where record traffic was recorded during the year. The ITF is committed to innovations that enhance the appeal of the event for fans and players alike, and the introduction of electronic line-calling technology for this year's final was the latest of these.

There are too many good stories from this year's competition for me to do them justice here, but in his third time writing this book, Chris Bowers looks in detail in the following pages at all the 2006 World Group and Play-off ties. His extensive research and interviews with the participants ensure that this is a comprehensive record of the Davis Cup year. Accompanying the text are the stunning photographs we have come to expect from the world's leading tennis photographers.

Congratulations to Russia for its second Davis Cup victory, and for ascending to the No. 1 spot on the ITF Davis Cup Nations Ranking. Thank you to all 133 nations that took part this year, and good luck for their campaigns in 2007.

Francesco Ricci Bitti
President, International Tennis Federation

SPONSOR OF TENNIS
EVERY KIND OF TENNIS

BNP PARIBAS

Giving tennis the advantage

FOR MORE THAN THIRTY-THREE YEARS NOW, BNP Paribas, one of the world's foremost banking groups and the number one bank in the euro zone, has chosen to support tennis.

Along with its 140,000 employees in eighty-five countries, BNP Paribas shares a number of core values with the sport, most notably keenness associated with a sense of discipline, performance allied with fair play, and a desire for recognition combined with a sense of tradition and elegance.

As the sponsor of "every kind of tennis," BNP Paribas:

- Encourages junior tennis through its support of Junior Fed Cup by BNP Paribas, Junior Davis Cup by BNP Paribas, and the BNP Paribas Cup (in conjunction with UNESCO).
- Provides substantial assistance in several of the eighty-five countries in which the bank is present, for educational tennis programs developed by national associations for amateur players of all ages.
- Supports sports outreach programs such as "Fête le Mur," a charitable organization founded by Yannick Noah that aims to promote social cohesion in underprivileged areas of France by involving disadvantaged youngsters in playing tennis.
- Is involved in wheelchair tennis as the title sponsor of the BNP Paribas Open de France, the French Open of the discipline.
- Partners tennis at a worldwide level through its close association with numerous elite tennis events—the French Open since 1973, the BNP Paribas Masters in Paris, the Monte Carlo Masters Series event, the Bank of the West Classic in California (Bank of the West is a BNP Paribas Company) and the Rome Masters Series event which in 2007 will become the Internazionai BNL d'Italia following the integration of the Banca Nazionale del Lavoro (BNL) into the BNP Paribas Group in 2006.
- Has, since 2001, been a proud member of the ITF family, sponsoring the world's largest team tennis competitions for men and women: Davis Cup by BNP Paribas and Fed Cup by BNP Paribas.

2006 has been a great year for the ITF's flagship competition, with the champion nation Russia being of significant importance to our business development strategy and having hosted both a magnificent semifinal and final. As the group prepares to launch a retail banking program in Russia, we could not have hoped for a better result.

That is to take nothing away from the runner-up, Argentina, a Davis Cup nation that is just as important to BNP Paribas. Argentina is a country where the bank hosts what is probably its strongest client hospitality program anywhere in the world, and whose national team has once again proved its class.

It is therefore with great pleasure that we take the opportunity with this book to relive this magnificent year of Davis Cup by BNP Paribas in words and photos. We hope that you enjoy it too.

Michel Pébereau

Michel Pébereau
Chairman, BNP Paribas

FOREWORD

IT WAS A GREAT PLEASURE TO BE A MEMBER OF THE RUSSIAN DAVIS CUP TEAM IN 2006 and to win the title. Never as a kid had I imagined I'd be part of a team, much less holding this trophy, but nineteen years into my tennis career I can finally say that it has happened.

All of my teammates had doubts and uncertainties about whether we would win the Davis Cup this year. With the Netherlands, France, USA, and Argentina in our way to the title, it's hard to say that our fears weren't valid. Looking back at the matches we played in 2006, sometimes I question how did we win? So many matches could have gone the other way, and that makes this Cup even more special. All of the countries mentioned gave us the ultimate test, and each test we faced and passed as a team. We stood by each other in the joy of winning and the pain of losing as one family, and regardless of the end result I feel that I found friends that no amount of time will erase from my memories.

Yes, it is a great honor to win the Davis Cup and to see your friends stand by your side and hold up the trophy along with you, but to give this victory to Russian fans and bring the Cup to our country is a humbling feeling that's hard to describe.

It is also a great honor to hear thousands of fans chanting, "Thank you!" Seeing them with tears of joy on their faces made me realize that this victory is so much more important than any personal win I ever had or will have in the future. Yes, we are athletes in an individual sport, but how many of our fans have dreamt of seeing the Russian team raise the Cup?

And it is a great honor to see the first president of Russia, Boris Yeltsin, the biggest and most prominent fan of our team, cheer on every point from one stand, and the equally distinguished Diego Maradona support the Argentines from the other. That proves people of all cultures, ages, and statures can come together to celebrate one of the greatest events in sports.

Finally, it is a great honor to be a part of all this and to realize that this is what you live for! For etching your name in history. For reaching a goal not just by yourself but with people that matter to you. For the fans, and for a sport that is truly able to unite masses.

It was heartbreaking to see Chucho in tears after the decisive match in the final, because all of us had felt the pain of a loss, and knew how it felt to give your everything and not win. Any of us could have ended up crying that week, and there is no shame in tears of that kind. Jose didn't turn down the responsibility and immense pressure of the last match and fought till the last point. He, David, Agustin, and Juan Ignacio deserved to win the Davis Cup just as much as we did, but this victory was for our fans. They needed to see their hopes come to life and, sometimes, that means much more than a personal triumph.

Dmitry Tursunov

INTRODUCTION

SEVERAL YEARS FROM NOW, a sports historian is likely to write a history of the golden era of Russian tennis in the first decade of the twenty-first century. In it, the Davis Cup by BNP Paribas of 2006 will merit a chapter of its own.

By the start of 2006, Russia needed no confirmation that, in terms of aggregate male and female performance, it was the leading global power in tennis. Its 2002 Davis Cup triumph had been followed by the Fed Cup in 2004, and a second Fed Cup title followed in 2005. In terms of rankings, Nikolay Davydenko had established himself in the world's top ten, Marat Safin was only out of it because of a series of injuries, and you couldn't move for Russians in the women's top ten.

What was missing was a home Davis Cup triumph. Mikhail Youzhny's heroic five-set victory over France's Paul-Henri Mathieu had taken place in Paris. Russia's women won in Moscow in 2004 and in Paris in 2005. The missing piece of the jigsaw was a home triumph for Russia's men. In 2006 they delivered it, and in almost as thrilling a fashion as their first triumph four years earlier.

Perhaps fittingly, everyone who was anyone in Russian men's tennis was there. Alex Metreveli, the most successful player in the history of the Soviet and Russian tennis team, was commentating for television and was a popular recipient of the 2006 Davis Cup Award of Excellence. Andrei Chesnokov, the architect of Russia's phenomenal semifinal victory over Germany in 1995 showed up, a little less hair on top but those eyes just as piercing as in his heyday. Olga Morozova, the first Russian woman to make it to a Grand Slam singles final, was there. And Yevgeny Kafelnikov, the first Russian to win a Grand Slam singles title and top the rankings, was also around, a little more portly than in his playing days but with the same boyish face and haircut, and proudly parading his two daughters.

But it wasn't just nostalgia. What Russia showed best of all was a squad ethic that cannot be measured but contributes to a team triumph. Igor Andreev played in the first round against the Netherlands but then needed knee surgery and played no further part—at least not on court. He was an unnominated member of the Russian squad for both the semifinal and the final, and was rewarded with a Davis Cup replica that was as much for his support as for playing in the first round. He shared the cheerleading and flag-waving duties with Mikhail Youzhny, who must have known he wouldn't play in the final after injuring his ankle in the St. Petersburg tournament in October, but was determined to be a squad player if not be present on court. Seeing the joy with which he sang the Russian national anthem after Marat Safin had beaten Jose Acasuso for the winning point made it seem as if he got more pleasure out of Russia's 2006 triumph than its 2002 effort. Then he was involved to a dramatic extent, winning the fifth rubber after being two sets down. This time he had time and space to enjoy the moment. And it would be wrong not to mention today's Russian tennis family, the Safins—with Marat on court, and sister Dinara and mother Rausa Islanova providing vociferous support from the sidelines.

This is the story of how Russia showed the sporting world that winning at team tennis requires more than just a few individuals turning out for a handful of matches. And it was no coincidence that the team that came so close to thwarting that second title was a nation that had made the sometimes painful transition from a group of individual stars who underachieved as a team, to a group of team players whose impact was greater than the sum of its parts.

Whatever Argentina goes on to achieve with its wealth of talent, 2006 was a breakthrough year. Three failed semifinals in four years had left the 1981 achievements of Guillermo Vilas and Jose Luis Clerc the benchmark for Argentinian Davis Cup success. Not since then had Argentina made it to the final, despite a depth of representation in the top 100 that most nations would kill for. On the twenty-fifth anniversary of Vilas and Clerc's valiant effort against the USA in Cincinnati, when they lost in the fourth rubber at the height of John McEnroe's career, the Argentinians made it to a second final. And by taking it to a fifth rubber, the nation came closer than ever to lifting Dwight Davis's trophy. It was as if the monkey of Vilas and Clerc's achievement had been lifted from their collective back.

It was in 2006 that the Grand Slam nations reestablished themselves after a poor 2005. Australia and the USA made it to the semifinals, while France was a quarterfinalist. But two nations were left with a sense of what might have been. Switzerland spent years hoping for a second singles player to back up Roger Federer—in 2006 it had one, only to find the great man didn't want to play in the first round; after February's defeat to Australia, Swiss involvement was limited to the play-off round. And 2005 champion Croatia could well have defended its title, were it not for a spasm in Mario Ancic's back that cropped up at the worst possible time: the day before Croatia's home quarterfinal against Argentina.

There was the usual crop of ranking-defying personal triumphs. Chris Guccione, a shy lefthander who couldn't get into the top 100, defied his ranking to win two crucial rubbers that helped see Australia through to the semifinals. And Dmitry Tursunov became an unlikely hero for the champions—three times a shock selection, three times he delivered the goods. Tursunov had moved from Moscow to California when he was twelve and might have turned into a full-fledged American had a nine-year application for a green card not been persistently turned down by U.S. officials. The Davis Cup helped Tursunov, a somewhat idiosyncratic individual who communicates much more freely via the written than the spoken word, to rediscover his Russian-ness. Asked in an interview with a French tennis magazine what he remembered of the 2002 final, Tursunov replied: "Nothing really, I just wasn't interested." Ask him what he remembers of the 2006 final, and Tursunov, whose laconic writing style charmed thousands of tennis fans in an Internet blog, will have a lot more to tell his grandchildren.

For Tursunov had discovered not just the Davis Cup by BNP Paribas, but also that indefinable extra dimension and responsibility that allows the competition to turn some boys into men, and some men into wrecks. ●

Pictured on previous page:

Marat Safin (RUS)

Pictured opposite from top:

The Russian team with the trophy; David Nalbandian (ARG)

first round 10–12 FEBRUARY

Croatia defeated Austria 3-2   GRAZ, AUSTRIA—INDOOR CLAY

Argentina defeated Sweden 5-0   BUENOS AIRES, ARGENTINA—OUTDOOR CLAY

Belarus defeated Spain 4-1   MINSK, BELARUS—INDOOR CARPET

Australia defeated Switzerland 3-2   GENEVA, SWITZERLAND—INDOOR CLAY

France defeated Germany 3-2   HALLE, GERMANY—INDOOR HARD

Russia defeated Netherlands 5-0   AMSTERDAM, NETHERLANDS—INDOOR CARPET

USA defeated Romania 4-1   LA JOLLA, CA, USA—OUTDOOR HARD

Chile defeated Slovak Republic 4-1   RANCAGUA, CHILE—OUTDOOR CLAY

David Nalbandian (ARG)

The French team at the official dinner;

Halle's Gerry Weber Stadium

FIRST ROUND

THIS WAS THE YEAR NORMAL SERVICE WAS SUPPOSED TO BE RESUMED. But after the upheavals of 2005, what was normal any more? Had Croatia and the Slovak Republic, champion and runner-up, just been lucky in 2005, or were they now members of the team tennis elite? With Romania, Belarus, and 2002 champion Russia also in the World Group, was the dominance of Eastern Europe set to get stronger after its superb year of 2005? And how strong were the traditional powerhouses of America, Australia, and France, all of which boasted quality players but had question marks hanging over their effectiveness as teams?

As if to provide another hoop to jump through after their heroics in 2005, the defending champion Croatia created waves in the run-up to the 2006 first round. What had seemed at the Davis Cup Final to be a natural captaincy succession, waiting to take place seamlessly, suddenly turned sour. The veteran Niki Pilic, who had made history by becoming the first man to captain two nations to victory (Germany and Croatia), was expected to step down and let Goran Ivanisevic take over. But expectation and predictability have never been words naturally associated with Pilic and Ivanisevic, and after a series of political ructions within Croatian tennis, it became clear neither man would captain Croatia in the defense of its title. But who would?

Into the breach stepped the Davis Cup by BNP Paribas player of 2005, Ivan Ljubicic. The man who played twelve live rubbers, winning eleven of them, volunteered for an additional task—that of playing captain. It seemed madness. After all, it had been eighty years since a defending champion had fielded a playing captain—could the tall Croat really sit through Mario Ancic's singles and then get up and play his own match? That was the plan. To some it seemed an unnecessary millstone around the young champions' necks, but if 2005 taught anyone anything, it was not to underestimate the competitiveness and team spirit of the Croats.

Another talking point in the run-up to the first-round ties was whether three of the biggest names in tennis would turn out for their countries. The nominated line-ups produced six of the world's top ten, an impressive percentage, but two were missing—the top two, Roger Federer and Rafael Nadal—plus the eleventh-ranked Lleyton Hewitt.

There's no question Nadal was champing at the bit to play. He had been out for three months with a bizarre foot injury, caused by an ill-fitting shoe that his clothing company (which pays him millions of dollars) had developed from photographs rather than arranging for him to have a fitting in person. Nadal's advisers told him that best-of-five-sets matches would be too much for his comeback event, so he made his comeback a week later—by which time Spain had been eliminated. Federer and Hewitt were missing for reasons that questioned their commitment to the competition they had been so passionate about two years earlier, though Hewitt did return in the quarterfinal round, and the fact that both were missing made the Switzerland v Australia tie the most exciting of the first round.

And then there was the question of Germany, returning to the World Group for the first time in three years. With Tommy Haas and Nicolas Kiefer both playing some of their best tennis at the same time, could the Germans become a power for the first time since the era of Boris Becker and Michael Stich? They were blessed with a home draw against the French, whose team still seemed somewhat in construction mode when the world's best sixteen nations lined up from Halle to La Jolla over the second weekend of February. ●

GERMANY v FRANCE

VIEWED FROM THE PERSPECTIVE OF 1995–96, no one should have been surprised to see Germany in the 2006 World Group, and as one of the outside favorites for the title.

In 1995, the Becker/Stich era was still in full swing. Becker was the Wimbledon runner-up in 1995 and the Australian Open champion in 1996. Stich, though troubled by injury, could still beat anyone on his day and was French Open runner-up in 1996. More important, Germany had a crop of promising youngsters coming through. Nicolas Kiefer and Ulrich Seetzen were two of the world's top juniors in 1995, and the following year, Daniel Elsner won two junior Grand Slam titles. The future looked bright for Germany's post-Becker/Stich era.

But it didn't quite work out. Kiefer broke onto the tour and reached fourth in the world rankings in 2000. But Seetzen and Elsner both fell by that tennis wayside that is littered with the unfulfilled careers of promising juniors. In their place, Tommy Haas, a youngster who had shown that it was possible to come through the Nick Bollettieri academy with a one-handed backhand, became Germany's most successful player since Becker and Stich, and Rainer Schuettler's supreme fitness propelled him to one outstanding year on the tour.

The problem for German team tennis was that the three never seemed to play well together, and Kiefer in particular had a Davis Cup record that didn't impress. When Kiefer was at his height in 2000, Haas was still coming up. When Haas reached No. 2 in the rankings in May 2002, Kiefer's ranking was down in the 70s. And when Schuettler was runner-up to Andre Agassi at the Australian Open in 2003 and went on to end the year sixth, Haas was recovering from shoulder surgery, which almost ended his career.

The result was that Germany spent three years in the Davis Cup wilderness—not that there is any discredit in being in Europe/Africa Zone Group I, but for a nation used to its role as a perennial bet to win the cup, being outside the World Group was bordering on a humiliation.

All of which explains why, at the start of 2006, there was real optimism in the German camp. Not only were the Germans back in the World Group, having beaten the Czech Republic in a marathon play-off tie the previous September, but Kiefer and Haas were finally playing well at the same time. Haas came into the Davis Cup first round as the newly crowned champion from Delray Beach the previous weekend—he had lost just twice in thirteen matches, both to Roger Federer, and had taken the great man to five sets in the fourth round at the Australian Open. Kiefer had also lost in Melbourne to Federer, but he had finally reached a Grand Slam semifinal at the thirty-fifth time of asking, and had beaten Sebastien Grosjean in the quarterfinals in a four-hour, forty-eight-minute thriller that seemed to give him a psychological advantage. With Alexander Waske, a late-blooming fast-court player whose passionate support for his country was as much part of his selection as his prowess as a doubles player (he said after the draw: "Don't think I have Friday and Sunday off—I have to support the team from the sidelines, and that's exhausting enough"), Germany had a well-balanced, in-form team.

Moreover, it was a team with home advantage against opponents in transition. Germany's players made a specific request for the Gerry Weber Stadium in Halle, where Haas, Kiefer, and Schuettler had all reached the semifinals or better at the grass court

Pictured from top:
Tommy Haas (GER), left, and Alexander Waske (GER);
Tommy Haas (GER)

GERMANY v FRANCE CONTINUED

tournament held there, and with newly installed heating, the 12,300-seat arena was able to host the tie under its retractable roof on a temporary hard court expected to suit the home team.

With Grosjean having done well in Australia, and the pairing of Arnaud Clement and Michael Llodra selecting themselves in doubles, Guy Forget's only major decision as French captain was who would play second singles. Richard Gasquet qualified on rankings—in fact, he was ranked above Grosjean—but had won only one match out of five coming in to the tie following a series of minor injuries in late 2005. Paul-Henri Mathieu traveled to Halle having done well in Melbourne, but another Melbourne quarterfinalist, Fabrice Santoro, didn't, having fallen out with his entire team after failing to attend a pre-tie training camp. As the players practiced with snow dropping gently onto the transparent roof above them, Forget plumped for Gasquet—and it proved to be the key decision of the weekend.

Those who made Germany the slight favorite seemed to have tennis logic on their side, but they proved less intuitive than those who devised the menu for the official tie dinner on the Wednesday night. In a gesture of supreme diplomacy, the starter wine was a German white, and the main course wine a French red. As the weekend evolved, the French red proved vastly more full-bodied than the somewhat pale German white whose taste never quite lived up to its bouquet.

The Kiefer-Grosjean opener was expected to be close, but when Grosjean won both the opening sets, he broke Kiefer's resistance. The score of 7–5 7–6(7) 6–0 doesn't lie, but the match time of two hours fifty-five minutes testifies to how close those first two sets were.

On a day in which the umpires and referee were involved somewhat more than anyone would have liked, there were two defining moments. The first came in the tenth game of the first set, when Kiefer had two set points. He had looked very nervous at the start, but had overcome that to put pressure on the Grosjean serve. This looked like his moment to strike. But Grosjean won four points on the run, broke Kiefer in the following game, and wrapped up a slow-moving first set 7–5.

The fluctuating encounter was effectively decided in the second-set tiebreak. But what the bare numbers cannot describe is the drama of the sixteenth and final point of the shootout, nor the fury Kiefer felt during and after the point that went against him. He had already saved two set points at 5–6 and 6–7. Having come back from 3–5 in games, he seemed to find the moment to turn the match his way. He and most of the nine thousand fans thought he had saved a third set point when Grosjean couldn't control his return off a fierce first serve. But the line umpire behind Grosjean had called the ball out, and though he corrected his call, the point had to be replayed. Kiefer was angry but could not complain. He pushed his second serve on the replayed point dangerously close to being a fault, and then watched helplessly as a Grosjean crosscourt return left him stranded. But was it in or out? The line umpire—a different one—started to call the ball out, but then changed his mind; umpire Mohammed Lahyani decided the changed call hadn't affected Kiefer and announced the set for Grosjean. Not that most people heard it, because for several minutes Kiefer and Germany's captain Patrik Kuehnen remonstrated furiously with Lahyani and the referee Mike Morrissey.

Pictured from top:

Left to right: referee Mike Morrissey, Nicolas Kiefer (GER) and German captain Patrik Kuehnen; Sebastian Grosjean (FRA)

Pictured opposite from top:

Richard Gasquet (FRA); Nicolas Kiefer (GER)

Pictured from top:

Richard Gasquet (FRA); France celebrates

Pictured opposite:

Michael Llodra (FRA), left, and Arnaud Clement (FRA)
are congratulated by their teammates

GERMANY v **FRANCE** CONTINUED

Television replays suggested the Grosjean return had been on the line. Regardless of the rights and wrongs, it broke Kiefer's resistance as Grosjean rolled through the third set in barely half an hour. To his credit, Kiefer said it would be wrong to say the whole match was decided by a bad call. "We played for nearly three hours," he said, "and it was very close. Obviously they were decisive points at the end of the tiebreak, but I never felt really comfortable out there, I could never get my distance to the ball right, but still there was a lot of high quality tennis in the match." He later revealed he was suffering from a foot injury that had restricted his practice time.

Going into the first day, the general feeling was that Germany would at worst be 1-1, as Haas was expected to have too much form for the still teenage Gasquet. And when the German took the first set 6-1, it looked to be an early night. But Gasquet is a quality player, and it was only going to be a matter of time before he rediscovered his world-beating form. With perfect timing, he chose that moment to rediscover it, to get the better of Haas in three of the remaining four sets.

A break early in the second set broke Haas's momentum, and by the time the match was level at one set all, Gasquet was playing the better tennis. He was playing with greater variety, mixing up serving-and-volleying with drop shots and deadly accurate backhands. In addition, his defense was superb, frequently putting shots played at full stretch into the last half-meter of Haas's court.

The real drama of the match came at the end of the third set. With Gasquet serving at 5-4, 30-30, a serve down the middle was called out but overruled by umpire Adel Aref. The crowd, already feeling Germany had had the worst of the decisions, was indignant, and barracked Gasquet during the following point. Though Haas won it, referee Morrissey adjudged the crowd to have hindered the Frenchman, and ordered the point to be replayed. This lit the blue touchpaper. There was booing and whistling, and a temporary state of stalemate. Eventually Morrissey persuaded Kuehnen to speak to the crowd via the umpire's microphone. "I've been asked by the referee to warn you to keep quiet during rallies," the German captain said. Opinions differed as to whether that choice of words was unstatesmanlike by clearly siding with the crowd, or well judged to have shown some understanding for the crowd's anger. Either way, it did the trick. Kuehnen went on to tell the fans that they risked costing Germany a point under the partisan crowd rule of the Davis Cup by BNP Paribas, and there was scarcely any further trouble all weekend.

Gasquet won the set, but Haas broke in the first game of the fourth. He seemed to be on the way back—only he wasn't. Gasquet broke back for 1-2 with the help of another overrule, one for which television replays offered no conclusive evidence. This finally broke Haas's cool and he earned a warning for an audible obscenity two points later. But Haas went on to lead 5-3 and the momentum seemed to be with him. Again it wasn't. Again he couldn't build on his lead, and it took a tiebreak for Haas to get into a fifth set.

Surely Gasquet would now tire, and Haas's streak of wins in the previous five weeks would come to his assistance? But no. Haas had expended so much energy getting back into the match that he hit the wall at the start of the fifth. By the time he got into his

stride he was hopelessly adrift. Saving two match points at 1–5 gave him short-term hope, but when Gasquet dived for a crosscourt forehand to win the match 1–6 6–4 6–4 6–7(1) 6–3 in three hours thirty-six minutes, the Frenchman had sealed a deserved victory.

He had also killed off the tie as a spectacle. While the doubles was always competitive, once the early momentum had worn off, there was a clear gap in class between the competent Haas and Waske, and the increasingly accomplished Clement and Llodra. Clement didn't play well, but Llodra abandoned his characteristic flamboyance to play a more solid game and carry his partner until the crucial stage of the match.

Having saved three set points, the Germans were delighted to win the first set on an 8–6 tiebreak. The French came into their own in the second, but when Germany broke to lead 4–3 in the third, a fightback was on. Yet that was the cue for France to reel off six games on the run, playing their best tennis of the match, punctuated by some quite superb defense in which Waske and Haas were forced to play shot after shot following apparent winners. As a way of breaking the opposing team's spirit, it was perfect, and the visitors wrapped up their quarterfinal place with a 6–7(6) 6–3 6–4 6–1 win.

For a tie expected to be so close, and with Germany the slight favorite, it was a shock result. But many were left wondering whether the French have cast a spell over their neighbors in team tennis. The two nations met in 1913 in the first-ever Davis Cup tie not to be played on grass. This was only their seventh subsequent meeting, and only their second in fifty years. Yet you have to go back to 1938 to find the last time Germany won even a live rubber against the French. "We haven't suddenly become a bad team," said Kuehnen after Germany had salvaged some pride by winning the dead rubbers. But his side had still to work out how to tackle the corporate French and their wily captain, Forget. ●

NETHERLANDS v **RUSSIA**

FRANCE'S WIN ROBBED RUSSIA OF A HOME QUARTERFINAL. The clear favorite against the Dutch, Russia would have hosted the Germans, but in the end found itself facing an away trip to the Pyrenees. Russia's first-round passage against the Dutch was as easy as it was expected, and it survived the injury curse of the Netherlands that had become so widespread even the Dutch had to laugh about it.

The Netherlands tennis scene was no place for the frail of body in February 2006. The country's top two players were both victims of long-term secondary injuries. Martin Verkerk had battled his way back from a second shoulder operation and was ready to make his comeback in January, only to be struck down by glandular fever. And Sjeng Schalken's chronic back injury had led to so many compensatory injuries that he had hit fewer balls than Verkerk—and all of them in practice.

At least the Dutch had Peter Wessels, their Davis Cup find of 2005, who was fully up for the tie against Russia. He was practicing to the maximum and playing some great tennis, but then, the day before the draw, he aggravated a chest muscle. He had first

Pictured from top:

Melle van Gemerden (NED); Dmitry Tursunov (RUS)

Pictured opposite:

Raemon Sluiter (NED)

Pictured from top:

Nikolay Davydenko (RUS); Raemon Sluiter (NED)

Pictured opposite from top:

The Russian team celebrates;

Mikhail Youzhny (RUS), left, and Igor Andreev (RUS)

NETHERLANDS v **RUSSIA** CONTINUED

aggravated it at the Hopman Cup five weeks earlier and had been encouraged to get it X-rayed, but as it seemed to recover within a couple of days, he assumed it was fine and carried on playing. That assumption cost the Dutch dearly. On the eve of the tie, an X-ray by the Dutch team revealed a slight tear, and Wessels was out of the tie.

The Netherlands' top three players were all out with injuries, and the following week the ATP tournament in Rotterdam saw thirteen players from a thirty-two-player field withdraw through injury. No wonder the Dutch tennis community began talking wryly about a Dutch disease.

For there to be any life in the Netherlands-Russia tie, Raemon Sluiter needed to win the opening singles against Dmitry Tursunov, the Russian playing his first live Davis Cup by BNP Paribas singles match. Sluiter is effectively "Mr Davis Cup" in his home country, the faithful Dutch having never forgotten his five-set win over Juan Carlos Ferrero in 2001 when Spain came to Eindhoven as defending champion and was beaten in two days. Sluiter rises to big occasions and had tried to temper his slight overexuberance by taking up meditation in the months leading up to the tie. Yet even playing his team's "must-win" rubber, he knew he was the underdog.

Tursunov came into the tie as the lowest-ranked of the four Russian players—at 50th. And he proved too good for Sluiter, though not before a nervous start had given the Dutchman hope. The expressive Sluiter took the first set on a tiebreak, and then when he broke back for 5–5 in the third set after Tursunov had served for a 2–1 lead, an unlikely home win suddenly looked possible. But Sluiter likes patient opponents who give him a nice rhythm, and the deceptively strong Tursunov goes for big winners at the earliest opportunities. That deprived Sluiter of a consistent ball, which in turn cost him dearly as the third set tiebreak neared its conclusion. Once the Russian had taken it, there was no way back for Sluiter, even if his big serve did manage to take the fourth set into a third breaker.

Though no one among the crowd of nine thousand in Amsterdam's RAI congress centre wanted to recognize it, Tursunov's 6–7(2) 6–4 7–6(5) 7–6(5) victory had finished the tie. Replacing Wessels in the second singles was Melle van Gemerden, the world No. 136 up against the fifth-ranked Nikolay Davydenko. Van Gemerden, who had beaten Davydenko twice in Challenger tournaments six years earlier, went out with nothing to lose, and played a fine first set, opening up a 4–2 lead. But it was a lot to ask to keep up such a level against the rock-steady Davydenko, and once the Russian had taken the first set on an 8–6 tiebreak, he cruised to a 7–6(6) 7–5 6–4 win.

The pairing of Igor Andreev and Mikhail Youzhny was thought to be the weakest of the combinations available to Russia's captain Shamil Tarpischev, but it was still too strong for Sluiter and John van Lottum. Van Lottum, another Dutch disease victim who was back in the national team following back surgery, played one of his better Davis Cup ties, but the wind was in the Russian sails, and Andreev and Youzhny booked their nation's place in the quarterfinals with a 6–2 3–6 6–4 6–4 win.

The irony for the Dutch was that their teams of the mid-2000s clearly had the one element that was missing from the Dutch teams of the 1990s: team spirit. In the 1990s the caliber of player available to Dutch captains was vastly higher, with Richard Krajicek,

NETHERLANDS v **RUSSIA** CONTINUED

Jan Siemerink, Paul Haarhuis, Jacco Eltingh, and Mark Koevermans forming a formidable pool of players. But Krajicek, the Wimbledon champion in 1996, could never produce his best form in the Davis Cup, and one semifinal in 2001 was all the great Dutch era had to show. With such injuries and little back-up, simply being in the World Group was a major achievement for the team spirit fostered by the Dutch captain Tjerk Bogtstra. But team spirit on its own was never going to beat the mighty Russians, even without Marat Safin. ●

SWITZERLAND v
AUSTRALIA

THE AGE OF THE MOBILE TELEPHONE hovered over the tie in Geneva's SEG Arena between Switzerland and Australia.

The build-up had been a case of "will he or won't he?" revolving around the three biggest names the two sides had to offer: Roger Federer, Lleyton Hewitt, and Mark Philippoussis. In the end all three didn't, but for different reasons. Federer had said the Davis Cup didn't figure as a top priority in his plans for 2006 so he would only play if it fit into his schedule. And after winning his first two tournaments of the year in Doha and Melbourne, where he was still not entirely free of residual pain in his right foot from a tendon tear four months earlier, he said he needed a break. Hewitt had an ankle problem, though his withdrawal was clouded with doubts about whether he had fallen out with the new regime at Tennis Australia, something his captain, John Fitzgerald, was keen to deny. And Philippoussis just wasn't selected—he had taken a wild card into the Australian Open in the hope of rediscovering some form, but had lost in the first round, and Fitzgerald felt the young crop of Australians were more deserving of a place in Geneva than the big-serving Melbournian.

Hewitt sent his good-luck messages before the tie, and that was largely it. But Federer, despite never setting foot in Geneva, was somehow present. The Swiss camp, led by the Czech-born German Ivo Werner as "Teamchef" and the captain Severin Luthi, decided Federer's experience would be welcome, even if only by phone. So on the practice days, the players were in regular contact with him by mobile phone, in one case with a group of players huddled around a phone switched to speakerphone, and throughout the weekend the players on the bench were regularly texting the absent world No. 1. A case of team spirit by SMS?

If the absence of Federer and Hewitt spoiled the spectacle for some, the fact that both were missing enhanced it as a contest—in fact, it was the only one of the eight first-round ties to go to a live fifth rubber. Yet there was a cruel irony for the Swiss. So often in the previous five years they had lost ties because there was no second player to win at least one point if Federer couldn't win all three himself. On this occasion Switzerland's No. 2 won both his singles—yet still the Swiss lost.

Stanislas Wawrinka had been one of the breakthrough players of 2005. He had played his first live Davis Cup singles eleven months earlier in another Federer-less team, as

Pictured from top:

Michael Lammer (SUI); Peter Luczak (AUS);

George Bastl (SUI), left, and captain Severin Luthi

Pictured opposite:

Stanislas Wawrinka (SUI)

SWITZERLAND v **AUSTRALIA** CONTINUED

Switzerland lost narrowly to the Netherlands. Facing an Australian singles line-up of Chris Guccione and Peter Luczak, the 51st-ranked Wawrinka dismissed both, but then had to do what Federer has so often had to—sit by as his team lost the tie on a fifth rubber.

In a weekend featuring five ties that were all 50/50 calls, Switzerland got the better start. Michael Lammer, a twenty-three-year-old from Zurich making his Davis Cup debut despite a ranking of 210, stormed to a 6–1 first set against a highly nervous Luczak, Australia's No. 1 after a run to the third round of the Australian Open had taken his ranking to 116. The cowbells were rung, the drums beaten, and the klaxons sounded—home advantage was becoming a tangible factor. But only for a set. Luczak, whose bleached blond hair tied back in a ponytail makes him look as if he's come straight off a New South Wales beach, found his range early in the second set, and the damage he did to Lammer's confidence in the remainder of the match played a role in who took part in the fifth and deciding rubber.

After Luczak's 1–6 6–3 6–0 6–3 win, Wawrinka was under some pressure against the big-serving left-hander Chris Guccione. Despite a slow indoor clay court, Guccione's accuracy meant the serve was always going to be effective, and when he levelled the match at a set all, Australia was looking comfortable. But Wawrinka's nerve held, and he took the match 7–5 3–6 6–4 7–6(6).

Having won in the singles, Switzerland decided to throw Wawrinka into the doubles instead of the previously nominated George Bastl. Though Wawrinka and Yves Allegro lost 7–6(6) 6–4 4–6 7–6(5) to the highly experienced pair of Wayne Arthurs and Paul Hanley, it showed Wawrinka's willingness to take on responsibility. Though Hanley was making his Davis Cup debut, he and Arthurs had played for many years together on the tour, and they were backed up by the doubles coaching skills of the sport's most successful doubles player, Todd Woodbridge. It was a high-quality match, in which Australia's doubles prowess just about made the difference.

Yet with Wawrinka still feeling fresh despite playing eight sets, all was not lost for the home nation. Wawrinka came out firing against Luczak, taking the first two sets comfortably, and setting up two match points in the third. When Luczak saved them and took the match into a fourth set, the cowbells were momentarily silenced, but it proved merely a blip, as the Swiss ended a highly creditable weekend for himself and set up the live fifth rubber.

Both captains could have made changes. After losing to Wawrinka on Friday, Guccione's confidence wasn't high, and the Aussies toyed with bringing in the thirty-four-year-old Arthurs, another big-serving left-hander who had reached the fourth round of the French Open in 2001. Switzerland had opted for the 210th-ranked Lammer on day one ahead of the higher-ranked Bastl (137), who, at age thirty, was less a choice for the future than Lammer but had played two live fifth rubbers and took them both to five sets: losing 6–4 to Mark Philippoussis in 2000 and 8–6 to Nicolas Escude in 2001. Lammer had had more matches in the run-up to the tie than Bastl, including a competent showing against world No. 3 Andy Roddick in Rod Laver Arena three weeks before, but his confidence was thought to be shaky. In the end Switzerland changed, and Australia stayed, so it was Bastl against Guccione.

It was to be the making of Guccione. On a slowish clay court, Bastl's ring rustiness left him ill equipped to handle a blistering serving display by the big left-hander. The Aussie fired down thirty-nine aces in a 7–5 6–3 7–6(7) win. He might almost regret Bastl having failed to

convert his set point in the third set, for a fourth set might easily have seen the twenty-year-old Melbournian get close to Joachim Johansson's record of fifty-one aces in a match—needless to say, Guccione saved that set point with an ace. Bastl created six break points, all of them in the first set, all of them saved with aces, and his third live fifth rubber was a third defeat as Guccione was left celebrating with a lap of honor.

Guccione's victory was a shot in the arm for the defenders of dead rubbers. Eleven months earlier, Australia had sealed victory over Austria in Sydney inside two days, and Peter Luczak was due to play the final rubber against Alexander Peya. But having already played once in Davis Cup, Luczak suggested Guccione should get the experience, so Guccione was thrown in, and promptly beat Peya 6–3 6–4. "Without that experience, I'm not sure I would have handled the crowd in Geneva the way I did," said Guccione. "I'm pretty calm, but when you've had ten thousand Aussies cheering for you as I'd had in Sydney, you know what you're playing for. It was such a proud moment for me."

Inevitably the Swiss were left wondering what might have been if Federer had made the short trip from his home in Basel. Two weeks later, Federer said: "If two or three people don't get it and criticize me, and two thousand get it and are okay with it, ..."—he let the sentence tail off, leaving the remainder blowing in the wind. And Wawrinka was quick to come to Federer's defense: "I'm very happy with the way these three days have gone," he said. "With all that Roger has already done for Switzerland, it's a bit too easy to criticize him for not being here." Maybe—it was just a shame that for the second year running, the world's best player by a long way took no active part in the Davis Cup by BNP Paribas World Group, despite his country being among the elite 16 nations. ●

BELARUS v SPAIN

SOME WOULD SAY IT WAS JUST MISFORTUNE, some would say it was the old Achilles Heel. Why did Spain, for all its dominance of the world's top 100, again prove to be a nation of poor travelers? In fairness, Rafael Nadal had a foot injury, Juan Carlos Ferrero had an abdominal muscle strain, and Carlos Moya had made it clear he would be unavailable for Davis Cup for at least the first half of 2006. But with more players in the top 100 than any other nation, why were the champions of 2000 and 2004 beaten inside two days by Max Mirnyi and Vladimir Voltchkov of Belarus?

A feature of Spain's two titles was its home advantage. In 2000 it was drawn at home in all four rounds, and in 2004 only had to travel in the first, when Nadal made his Davis Cup debut in a fifth-rubber win over the Czech Republic. But away from Spanish clay the nation resembles frightened rabbits, and though home advantage counts for a lot in the Davis Cup by BNP Paribas, the Spaniards looked lost without a phrasebook against the two-man team that has taken Belarus to the limit of its potential in tennis's premier team competition.

It was a rough baptism for Emilio Sanchez as Spain's new captain, but while the result continued to pile the pressure on the Spaniards' fragile away reputation, it was a triumph for what playing for your country can do for a player of talent but poor consistency.

Pictured from top:

Max Mirnyi (BLR); David Ferrer (ESP)

Voltchkov proved his ability when he reached the Wimbledon semifinals in 2000. Given his subsequent tour form, it was a freakish run, but it told him he could hold with the best on any given day, even if he couldn't do it on a regular basis. To that extent his victory with a ranking of 292 against the tenth-ranked David Ferrer was somewhat less of a shock, especially allowing for the fact that Ferrer was making his Davis Cup debut in an away tie on a quick indoor carpet court.

Yet the most impressive aspect of Voltchkov's 6–3 6–4 6–3 win on the opening day was that his level never let up. He barely missed a volley in two hours of play, while all the time the Spanish camp waited for the letdown they felt had to come. Yet it didn't, and Voltchkov's win proved the crucial rubber of the weekend.

He was buoyed by going into his match with Belarus 1–0 up, after Mirnyi had beaten Tommy Robredo 6–3 6–7(5) 6–3 6–3. Mirnyi delivered a high-powered serving display, which meant he always had Robredo under pressure on the Spaniard's service games. The result was a blow to Robredo, who had looked to be the best of the Spaniards in practice.

Then came Voltchkov's tour de force, and once he had won, it was hard to see a way back for the Spaniards. Mirnyi and Voltchkov are a seasoned doubles team, while Spain has struggled in recent years to find a reliable doubles pair. Emilio Sanchez opted for the all-left-handed combination of Feliciano Lopez and Fernando Verdasco, who are good friends and reached the quarterfinals of the 2005 US Open. The pair didn't play badly, but at the sharp end of all three sets, they were outplayed by a better unit. The first set went to the tiebreak, but the home pair had been ahead early and made Lopez look vulnerable on serve. A break in the ninth game of the second set gave the hosts a two-set lead, and a break in the eleventh game of the third set saw Belarus through to the last eight.

Thus was another chapter written in the remarkable story of the two-man Belarus golden era. And not surprisingly, the politicians were keen to be associated with the success. After Belarus had wrapped up victory, the country's president, Alexander Lukashenko, who was campaigning for a presidential election the following month, made an on-court presentation of a pistol to Mirnyi—no doubt a symbolic gesture for all the bullets Mirnyi had shot at the Spaniards with his big serve. ●

USA v ROMANIA

ONE OF THE BEAUTIES OF THE DAVIS CUP by BNP Paribas is that it takes top-level tennis to places that wouldn't otherwise see it. La Jolla, at the southern tip of southern California, which hosted the USA v Romania first round tie, is one such example.

Seldom can the tennis world have seen such a picturesque venue. In one direction from the La Jolla Beach and Tennis Club, you have the shimmering waters of the Pacific Ocean easing into an infinite horizon, punctuated by spectacularly mountainous promontories jutting out into the sea. In the other, you have the gentle slope of the hills as they roll down to the sea, a smattering of well-to-do houses carved into opportune crevices, the sun glinting off the occasional window to provide a sparkle against the

Pictured from top:

Max Mirnyi (BLR), left, and Vladimir Voltchkov (BLR);

Tommy Robredo (ESP)

backdrop of a dour green-brown landscape. Above, clear blue skies. And around the temporary stadium built for the tie, palm trees rustled in the breeze. It was almost as if, for one weekend, La Jolla was saying to the most spectacular regular venue on the professional tour, the Monte Carlo Country Club: we can do just as well as you.

For many of the six thousand or so members of the La Jolla tennis community who showed up for the weekend's action, such splendid scenery is part of their everyday reality. But as the Davis Cup show left town, they were left with the memories of having seen a festival of tennis—including a return to unofficial Davis Cup action by John McEnroe—in which the USA just about scraped into the quarterfinals, but not without a fair bit of luck.

There was no way the home team was going to take their Romanian opponents lightly. Eleven months earlier, one of the best American teams ever assembled had gathered just up the coast in Los Angeles to play Croatia—and suffered a humiliating defeat. The humiliation paled somewhat in the subsequent months as Croatia proved itself a genuine Davis Cup power and won the cup, but the memories of unexpected defeat were still fairly fresh in the U.S. psyche. And in a neat twist, the U.S. would have hosted Romania in the 2005 quarterfinals had they beaten Croatia, so to some, this tie was seven months late.

The home team suffered a minor blow in the days leading up to the tie with the absence of a familiar figure. Dean Goldfine had been a regular in Patrick McEnroe's set-up for four years, first under the USTA's auspices, then as personal coach to Andy Roddick. But the U.S. No. 1 split from Goldfine after his defeat to Marcos Baghdatis at the Australian Open, so Goldfine was out of the Team USA picture for the first time since 2002, and Roddick brought along his elder brother John.

Seldom can so many brothers have been formally involved in a single tie. As well as John Roddick, the USA's No. 2 player James Blake was without his longtime coach Brian Barker, so he brought along his elder brother Thomas. The identical twins, Bob and Mike Bryan, made up the U.S. doubles pairing, and Patrick McEnroe had his elder brother John in the commentary box—and later alongside him on court. Given that the USA's fifth (non-nominated) player was Mardy Fish, who had been a lodger with the Roddicks in his junior days, the Americans were very much keeping it in the family.

But the Romanians weren't going to be polite guests at a family celebration. They had come to spoil the party, and the fact that their most experienced player, Andrei Pavel, had seen his ranking slip to the point where he was No. 2 in his team (ranked 82nd behind the 41st-ranked Victor Hanescu) helped the visitors' chances. For Pavel knew exactly what to do in the first rubber when it became clear Roddick was ailing.

Roddick, who had been mobbed by female soldiers at the draw ceremony staged at the La Jolla marine base the day before, cruised to a two-set lead in the opening rubber. But early in the third came signs that his insides weren't playing as well as he was. As his strength ebbed, he held on into a third-set tiebreak. At 7-6 he had a match point on his own serve, but the previous five points had gone against the serve, and so did this as Pavel played a beautiful forehand lob to level at 8-8. When Pavel converted his fifth set point—two had come at 5-4 on the Roddick serve—he was into the match, and Roddick

Pictured opposite from top:

La Jolla Beach and Tennis Club;

Andy Roddick (USA), left, and captain Patrick McEnroe

Pictured from top:

Andrei Pavel (ROM); James Blake (USA)

began to slip out of it. "That tiebreak was the key to the match," Pavel said later.

After a game of the fourth set, Roddick vomited and took a medical timeout. After the first game of the fifth he vomited again and could have been forgiven for quitting. But in a supreme effort that he might not have made if playing only for himself, he forced his way back from 1–5 down to 4–5, before Pavel finally served out a 6–7(2) 2–6 7–6(8) 6–2 6–4 victory.

"It's the worst I've felt after a match," said Roddick, who was taken from the court and put on an intravenous drip. "I just went and laid down. Moving my leg or trying to get up off the floor felt like a mission. I've cramped before, but even while I'm cramping I've still felt like I had energy. Today, I just felt drained."

One point to Romania, and possibly more. Though Roddick said he was determined to play on Sunday, he clearly wouldn't be at his best, and with Victor Hanescu likely to face him in the fourth rubber, the Romanians were suddenly confident about a second successive quarterfinal.

But Hanescu ran into the true strength of the U.S. team: the esprit de corps. Though not the most successful Davis Cup captain when compared with the likes of Tony Trabert, Arthur Ashe, Tom Gorman, and others, Patrick McEnroe had done more than many of his illustrious predecessors to foster a team spirit. Roddick paid tribute to it at the draw ceremony, and in Roddick, Blake, and the Bryans, it's hard to think of a more team-orientated American line-up. Others may have won more Grand Slam titles, but seldom in the Open Era has an American team consisted of so many players who love other team sports and revel in the team variant of tennis.

With Roddick having lost, Blake was determined to show that he could be relied on to play his part. And he delivered one of his best Davis Cup displays to beat Hanescu 6–4 7–6(5) 6–2 to make a little history—it was the USA's two hundredth Davis Cup win in a series dating back to the first-ever rubber in the 106-year-old competition. "I tried not to get too emotionally involved in Andy's match," Blake said. "I kind of just let it roll off my back when he's losing, I just tell myself it doesn't change my job."

The Romanians never seriously thought they could win the doubles. The Bryans had come to La Jolla fresh from their third Grand Slam title at the Australian Open. They have a highly impressive Davis Cup record, but not for the first time the opposition they faced was less than it might have been. With Pavel and Hanescu nominated, Romania took a tactical decision to rest Pavel for a possible live fifth rubber, and replace him with Horia Tecau, a former ITF Junior Doubles World Champion. They should perhaps have gone all the way and rested Hanescu too, for a freak injury to the top-ranked Romanian in the first set of the doubles effectively decided the entire weekend.

Hanescu was serving at 2–4 deuce in the opening set when he held his left side and then took a medical time-out. He had torn ligaments in his left rib area. He returned to the court but lost the next two points, double-faulting to lose serve and put the Romanians behind 5–2 in the set. When Mike Bryan held his serve to take the first set 6–2, Hanescu realized his cause was hopeless, and Romania conceded the doubles. More important, he was clearly going to miss the first reverse singles, making Roddick's task a lot less frightening.

To fill the gap for the Saturday crowd, John McEnroe was hastily pulled out of the commentary box and dragged onto court to partner his younger brother against the Bryans in an eight-game exhibition match. The crowd loved it, and for many, the chance to see Roddick, Blake, the Bryans, and the McEnroes was a better deal than to have had a full-length doubles.

Not that Romania was fully out of it. Hanescu was clearly out of the first reverse singles, to be replaced by Razvan Sabau, the twenty-eight-year-old who had come back from two sets and 1–5 down to beat Great Britain's Jeremy Bates on his Davis Cup debut twelve years earlier. If he could find some of his best form against a subdued Roddick, then another landmark victory in an otherwise disappointing career was on the cards.

But Sabau couldn't make anything of his opportunity, and Roddick played a sensibly conservative match to see him to a 6–3 6–3 6–2 victory. It was the sixth time he had sealed victory for his country, and the sixth time the U.S. had beaten Romania in six meetings. In the end, Romania opted not to play Pavel in the fifth rubber, Blake beating Tecau in two straight sets.

No team likes to hit peak in the first round, and in the end it proved a fairly comfortable victory for the thirty-one-time champions. But the Romanians rode off into the sunset of the beautiful La Jolla aware that a run of better luck might have seen them inflict the kind of havoc Croatia had wrought eleven months earlier. ●

CHILE v SLOVAK REPUBLIC

THE AMERICANS KNEW A WIN WOULD GIVE THEM A HOME QUARTERFINAL, and it always looked likely to be against Chile, who had home advantage against a depleted Slovak side that had enjoyed four home ties in its run to the 2005 final. And like the USA with La Jolla, the Chileans decided to make top-level tennis reach a part of the world it had never reached before.

With Chile struggling to find tennis venues—indeed venues for any sport outside football—with a capacity of more than six thousand, it did a deal with the National Rodeo Federation to take the home Davis Cup by BNP Paribas tie to the prestigious Medialuna rodeo arena in Rancagua, about one hundred kilometers south of the capital, Santiago. The move mirrored Spain's choice of the Alicante bull ring for its semifinal against France in 2004, and with courtside seats swelling capacity, the venue could hold twelve thousand spectators. (Chilean rodeo is much less brutal than Spanish bullfighting—two men on horses have to push a cow onto a cushioned wall, and the cow lives to tell her friends about it.)

The result was one of the best atmospheres ever created for tennis in Chile. It was the first time the people of Rancagua had had the chance to see their Olympic heroes Nicolas Massu and Fernando Gonzalez ply their trade, and with temporary floodlights adding to the arena's existing lighting, play began at four in the afternoon on the Friday and seven in the evening on Saturday, thereby providing primetime entertainment.

If the one-sided nature of the score made the tie less attractive for the neutrals, it

Pictured from top:

Michal Mertinak (SVK); the Medialuna rodeo arena;

Fernando Gonzalez (CHI)

certainly didn't take anything away from the home team's delight. Not since 1982 had Chile won a World Group tie, and the end of twenty-four years of waiting was as fiercely celebrated after the doubles as it would have been if the third day's matches had been live.

With Karol Beck still under the shadow of a positive doping test (one that led to a two-year ban just days after the tie ended) and Karol Kucera having retired, it was a weakened version of the 2005 Davis Cup runners-up that represented the Slovak Republic' in Rancagua. Even the team captain, Miloslav Mecir, couldn't travel because of a back injury. Michal Mertinak, the twenty-six-year-old who had acquitted himself so well in losing the live fifth rubber of the 2005 final to Mario Ancic, was given a first-day singles slot despite having only arrived three days earlier from the European indoor circuit. Despite the adjustment from indoor hard court in winter to outdoor clay in summer, he took the world No. 15 Fernando Gonzalez to two tiebreaks in the opening rubber, before the home player won 7–6(5) 7–6(3) 6–3.

If the Slovak Republic was to have any chance of a win, Dominik Hrbaty had to beat Massu in the second singles. In a match lasting a minute short of four hours, Hrbaty got the better of the first set, and looked good at the start of the second. Then Gonzalez came out to join his teammates after showering and giving interviews following his match. At the first change of ends he picked up a water bottle and began beating a drum with it. The home supporters saw that as their cue, they got right behind their man, and Massu was visibly lifted.

Massu turned the match around in the second set, and then stormed through the third. Hrbary bounced back in the fourth and led for most of it, but as an elbow problem began to worsen, Massu clawed his way back into the set. It went into the tiebreak, the home player claiming it 7–4 for a 6–7(5) 6–3 6–1 7–6(4) triumph.

Much as Chile's captain Hans Gildemeister, who played in Chile's other World Group win over Romania in 1982, tried to say it wasn't all over, effectively it was. For the effort against Massu had taken its toll on Hrbaty's elbow, and he had to withdraw from the doubles. In his place came an eighteen-year-old, Lukas Lacko, who made a highly impressive debut alongside Mertinak, to suggest the Slovaks have a talent for the future. But against the Olympic gold medalists, they never seriously had a chance.

Showing few nerves, Lacko played so well it was Mertinak who was the weak link. Finally in the third set Mertinak picked up his level, and the match became a contest. But by then Gonzalez and Massu were two sets up, and while the visitors took the third, the match—and the tie—were soon over, the Chileans winning 6–2 7–5 3–6 6–4.

From 1986 to 2004 Chile was absent from the Davis Cup World Group, despite having the highly talented Marcelo Rios for much of that time. But Rios could never find someone with whom to share the load, whereas Gonzalez and Massu have both come good at the same time. "We have been playing for many years, Fernando and I," said Massu, "and when we started we never thought we would get so many things for our country playing as a team." Gonzalez added: "This result shows the maturity reached by the team, and we will go for more, we want more. This team can do it, and we will try to go for the Davis Cup."

Pictured from top:

The Slovak bench cheers its doubles team;

Dominik Hrbaty (SVK); Nicolas Massu (CHI)

Pictured opposite:

Nicolas Massu (CHI), left, and Fernando Gonzalez (CHI)

At the time they secured their quarterfinal place, the outcome of the USA-Romania tie was still uncertain. Within twenty-four hours it was clear that the Chileans would have to travel to America—and within a week it was clear they would have to dust off their grass-court shoes for the first time since Wimbledon the previous year. ●

AUSTRIA v CROATIA

IT COULDN'T REALLY HAPPEN, COULD IT? A PLAYING CAPTAIN? And a playing captain who was world No. 6, his country's top player and talisman, and taking the defending champions into a tough away match just two months after winning the Davis Cup? What would he do? Just the speeches at the official dinners and the captain's interview at press conferences, or would he actually sit on the bench?

All these questions surrounded Croatia's decision to have Ivan Ljubicic, the Davis Cup by BNP Paribas star of 2005, as playing captain for Croatia's first tie of 2006. And indeed he did what a captain should do: sat on the bench during Mario Ancic's opening singles against Jurgen Melzer, then played his own singles. Madness surely? Ljubicic would agree, but it worked.

The background is both simple and complex. Having created history in December 2005 by becoming the first captain to win the Davis Cup with two nations, Niki Pilic stepped down. Goran Ivanisevic was widely expected to take over, but for a series of unexplained reasons that should come as no surprise to those who know the so-called Split Personality, he said he wasn't ready to take over.

"Because we won the Davis Cup, I didn't want anyone new in the team," said Ljubicic of the coherent unit that had won the Davis Cup for the young Balkan nation. "I wanted the atmosphere to stay the same. In Austria it worked very well, but it's really hard because I have a lot of media things as captain, as a player, a lot of pressure also from the players because they always ask something."

On the eve of the tie, Ljubicic had tried to play down the captain's role. "I don't think it's a big deal," he had said, "most of the time we play alone and need to find our solutions alone." He was more concerned about the quality of the locker rooms in Graz's Schwarzl Freizeit Zentrum, which he said were "not up to World Group standard."

For his first match as playing captain, Ljubicic would probably have wished for a shorter match than the four-and-a-half hours he had to sit through. To be fair, he didn't sit through it all. "I stayed for one and a half sets. Then I went back to the locker room, had lunch, came back on court, stayed until about five games in the fifth set, by which time Mario was a break up. Then I came back to the locker room to prepare for my match."

For Ancic, it was another Davis Cup triumph following his live fifth rubber win two months earlier that had given Croatia the title. Never before had he come from two sets down, and this on his least favorite surface. Melzer seemed to have claimed the most significant two games, when he saved a set point in the twelfth game of the second set and then went on to win the tiebreak 7–4 to go two sets up.

But Ancic was not going to give up, and when he broke to lead 3–2 in the third set,

Pictured from top:

Stefan Koubek (AUT); Jurgen Melzer (AUT)

Pictured opposite from top:

Playing captain Ivan Ljubicic (CRO), left, and Mario Ancic (CRO);

Left to right: Julian Knowle (AUT), captain Thomas Muster

and Jurgen Melzer (AUT)

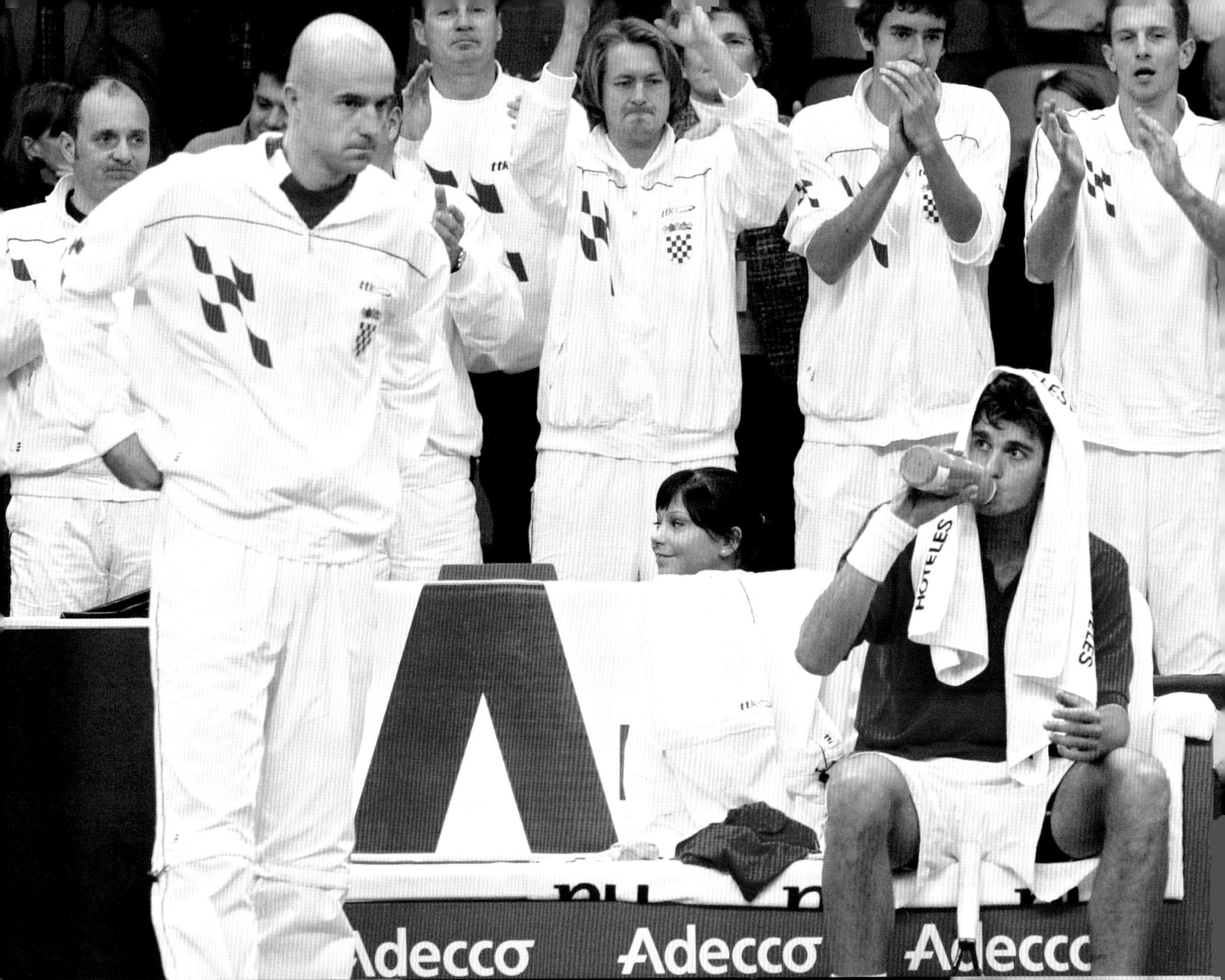
HOTELES
Adecco
Adecco

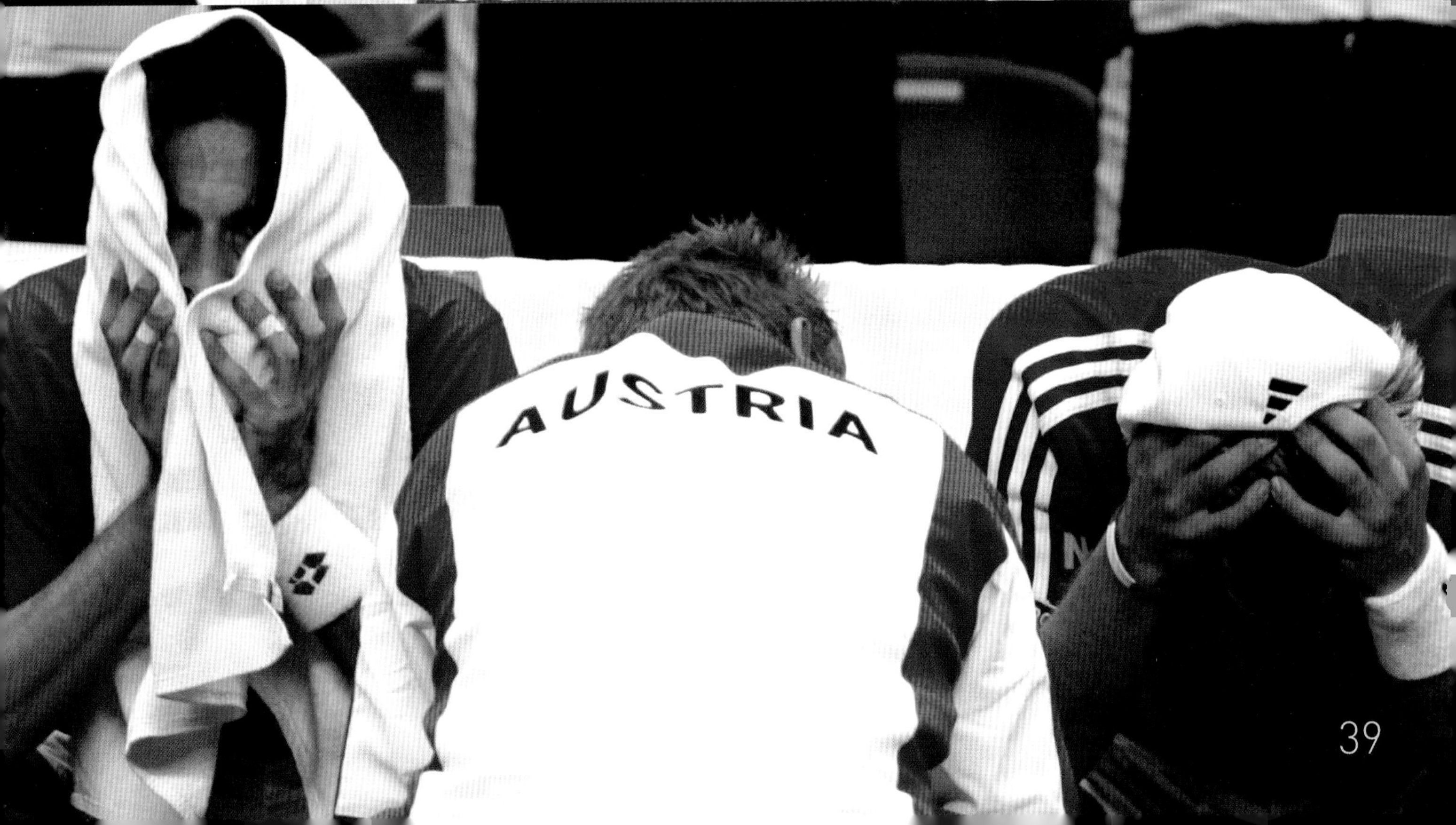
AUSTRIA

the match began to turn. Melzer had his chances, but whenever they arose, Ancic delivered a big serve to snuff out the danger. And early breaks in the fourth and fifth sets meant Melzer was always chasing the game. Ancic broke for the sixth time in the match to seal what he described as "one of my best Davis Cup wins, possibly the best one" before adding quickly: "If we win the tie."

So what would all the waiting and concentrating on Ancic's match do for Ljubicic? Well it certainly didn't hinder him. He had beaten Stefan Koubek in the final of the Zagreb tournament five days earlier, but that was on a hard court that favors Ljubicic—this was clay on which Koubek was more at home. You'd never have known it, though.

Ljubicic dropped just eight games in a 6–2 6–2 6–4 win that made him look like the home player. Koubek admitted he "never got going," but Ljubicic said too much was made of his supposed discomfort on clay. "Austrians may not know," he said, "but this is the ideal clay court for me—a slow, indoor court, the ball bounces high above the waist, like in Hamburg, and I've reached the semis in Hamburg. If you serve well, a clay court is no problem. For me, everything was perfect."

It was even more perfect after the doubles, by which time Croatia had become the first defending champions for three years to survive the following year's first round. But Ancic and Ljubicic had to do it the hard way. For the second day running Ancic had to come back from two sets down, as the Croatian pair beat Julian Knowle and Melzer 3–6 3–6 6–4 6–4 8–6 in four hours and five minutes.

The Austrians seemed to be cruising to a straight-sets win when Melzer was broken in the tenth game of the third set. A break in the tenth game of the fourth set took the match into a deciding set, which was packed with drama. Ancic served for the match at 5–3, but some great returning allowed the Austrians to break. Croatia had two match points at 6–5, but some great reflex volleying by Knowle kept the Austrians alive. At 6–6 Austria had a break point, but this time Ancic pulled off a great reflex volley. At 6–7, Melzer lost his serve from 40–0 up, leaving his captain Thomas Muster scratching his head in frustration. "It should have been 2–1 to us," he said, "but instead it's 3–0 for them. I guess that's life."

The 3–0 scoreline enabled Croatia to blood two youngsters who might have a role to play in the future, Ivan Cerovic and the junior world No. 1 Marin Cilic. Both lost, but both now know what the Davis Cup atmosphere is all about. ●

ARGENTINA v SWEDEN

THERE WAS A TIME IN THE 1990S WHEN SWEDEN HAD TWO DAVIS CUP TEAMS. One was for faster surfaces and included players such as Stefan Edberg, Jonas Bjorkman, and Thomas Enqvist. The other was wheeled out whenever the Swedes were playing on clay, headed by Magnus Gustafsson and Magnus Norman. How the seven-time champions would have loved a specialist clay court team to take to Argentina!

In recent years, Argentina has been almost invincible on its home clay but distinctly vulnerable when playing away. Not since September 1998, when Slovakia scored an

Pictured opposite:

Ivan Ljubicic (CRO); Mario Ancic (CRO)

Pictured from top:

Argentinian fans; Robin Soderling (SWE);

Jose Acasuso (ARG)

Pictured from top:

Jonas Bjorkman (SWE), left, and Simon Aspelin (SWE);

Thomas Johansson (SWE); Argentinian celebrations

Pictured opposite:

David Nalbandian (ARG)

ARGENTINA v SWEDEN CONTINUED

impressive victory in Buenos Aires, had the Argentinians lost at home, and even with Guillermo Coria and Gaston Gaudio both injured, the home nation had such a wealth of talent to call on that there was no perceptible weakening of the team.

Coria was never nominated. Gaudio was, but then suffered a rib injury that caused him to pull out in the week of the tie. Into the breach stepped Jose Acasuso, the freshly crowned champion from the ATP event in Vina del Mar, Chile, who was up to a career-high ranking of 33. Argentina's only weakness seemed to come in the doubles, where the search was once again on for a partner for the highly versatile David Nalbandian.

For only the ninth time since Argentina entered the Davis Cup in 1923, it hosted a home tie away from the Buenos Aires Lawn Tennis Club, the traditional home of Argentinian tennis. Thanks to a deal with an industrialist and the Buenos Aires city council, a temporary stadium was built in the Parque Julio Roca, an unused area on the south side of the capital next to the Buenos Aires Formula 1 motor racing track. The stadium offered a capacity of 10,300 spectators, over 4,000 more than the Buenos Aires LTC, and the Argentinian tennis authorities were hoping the stadium could become permanent and even host a national training center.

The chances of that happening would clearly be enhanced by a home win, which was always in the cards. Nalbandian could even afford one of his characteristic slow starts in the opening rubber, dropping the first set to Robin Soderling before bouncing back to win in four. Watched by a capacity crowd that included the former Argentinian football star Diego Maradona, Nalbandian took a set to get his tactics right, but once he had claimed the third, Soderling never stood much of a chance, Nalbandian winning 3-6 6-2 6-4 6-1.

All was not lost for Sweden, who fielded the 12th-ranked Thomas Johansson in the second rubber against Acasuso. Though clay is not his favorite surface, Johansson was expected to have a little too much experience for Acasuso—yet he won just five games. Making one of the more impressive Davis Cup debuts, Acasuso stormed through the match 6-1 6-1 6-3, overpowering Johansson from the baseline and making great use of his one-handed, down-the-line backhand. "I was completely stunned by Acasuso's game," Johansson said. "There was nothing I could do. I believed in the third set I could take the lead after breaking his serve, but he never budged."

The clay ought to have played less of a role in the doubles, in which Sweden were able to field the experienced Jonas Bjorkman and Simon Aspelin against Nalbandian and Agustin Calleri, who were playing together for only the third time. But momentum counted for more than experience, as the home pair ran out a 6-2 7-6(4) 2-6 6-4 winner to seal an away quarterfinal against Croatia. After an awful first set, Sweden came back to lead with a break early in the second, but once they had lost the tiebreak the Argentinian pair grew in comfort and confidence, and cruised to victory despite the blip of losing the third set.

Argentina's superb home record had continued, but now the most successful of the South American nations had discovered a new venue. All it needed was another tie. A home semifinal against Australia loomed as a distinct possibility—but standing in the way was the Croatian team that was happily showing the world that its victory in 2005 was no fluke. Croatia v Argentina would be one of the ties of the quarterfinal round. ●

FLYING THE FLAG

Country colors are proudly displayed in the Davis Cup by BNP Paribas,
from flags to playing kit down to the tiniest detail.

Name
CHRIS GUCCIONE

Born
30 JULY 1985 IN
MELBOURNE, AUSTRALIA

Turned professional
2003

A red-headed
Australian lefthander
with a great
temperament when
playing for his country.
Ring any bells?

PLAYER OF THE ROUND

CHRIS GUCCIONE HAS HAD TO DEAL WITH PLENTY of comparisons between himself and the great Rod Laver, with whom he shares his nationality, playing arm, and hair color. But while it's highly unlikely the Victorian will ever emulate the historic achievements of the Queenslander, he does have one advantage over Laver—his height. At two meters exactly (6 feet 7 inches), he stands head-and-shoulder-blades above the 1.72-meter Rockhampton Rocket, and possesses a blistering serve that Laver would love to have had.

The grandson of Italian immigrants who originally settled in Perth, Guccione first received the call-up to the Australian Davis Cup by BNP Paribas squad for the first round tie against Austria in 2005. He was something of a late developer—he began playing tennis at age eight at the Green Vale Tennis Club in Melbourne, and by fourteen was nothing special. But at sixteen he had a spurt in form, and at seventeen he surged to the final of the Wimbledon junior tournament, losing to Romania's Florin Mergea. Twenty months later he was in the Davis Cup fold.

An internal discussion among the Australian players gave Guccione his debut. With Australia 4–0 up against Austria and one dead rubber to play, Wayne Arthurs offered his place to "Gucc" to make his debut. "It was a great gesture," Guccione recalls, "and it gave me the experience to know I could go out and do it for my country."

That experience proved vital when a decidedly second-string Australian team traveled to Geneva in February 2006 to take on Switzerland. Australia's captain, John Fitzgerald, had to choose two singles players out of Arthurs, Peter Luczak, and Guccione. He resisted the temptation to go with Arthurs's experience, and plumped for the two younger guys who had played more on clay than many were aware of. "I'd had some good results on clay," says Guccione, "I'd won one Challenger tournament, I'd qualified and won a round at Roland Garros, so I knew how to play on clay."

He had to give second-best to Stanislas Wawrinka on the opening day in Geneva, but then found himself holding his nation's 2006 Davis Cup future in his hands in a live fifth rubber against George Bastl. Again Fitzgerald could have called on the experience of Arthurs for the crunch match—after all, Arthurs had reached the fourth round at the French Open in 2001—but he opted for Guccione. And Guccione delivered.

"In the run-up to that match [as Wawrinka was beating Luczak to set up the decisive rubber], I was so excited but also had such nerves," Guccione says. "I couldn't sit still, my palms were sweaty, I was watching the winter Olympics on the television, not the tennis."

But when he came out on court, he thundered down thirty-nine aces in three sets to blow Bastl away and send Australia into a quarterfinal in his home city of Melbourne. He was left doing a solitary lap of honor with the Australian flag around the SEG Geneva Arena. "It was such a proud moment, to have won for my country—it takes some beating."

Maybe Guccione did beat it in his win over Max Mirnyi in the quarterfinals, but that was the opening rubber. To have won a live fifth rubber in a World Group tie away from home really had lifted Guccione into rare and exalted company. ●

quarterfinals <small>7-9 APRIL</small>

Argentina defeated Croatia 3-2   ZAGREB, CROATIA—INDOOR CARPET

Australia defeated Belarus 5-0   MELBOURNE, AUSTRALIA—OUTDOOR HARD

Russia defeated France 4-1   PAU, FRANCE—INDOOR CARPET

USA defeated Chile 3-2   RANCHO MIRAGE, CA, USA—OUTDOOR GRASS

Pictured on previous page:
Fernando Gonzalez (CHI)
Pictured from top:
Mario Ancic (CRO); Jose Acasuso (ARG), left,
and David Nalbandian (ARG)
Pictured opposite:
Juan Ignacio Chela (ARG)

QUARTERFINALS

IT'S ALWAYS AROUND THE QUARTERFINAL ROUND THAT THOSE HEAVILY INVOLVED in the Davis Cup by BNP Paribas fall victim to a strange disorder, which weaves them into a string of potentially useful but utterly unreliable permutations.

This disorder is characterised by statements such as: "If country A beats country B, and country C beats country D, then A would be home to C in the semifinals, and if it then played country F in the final, it would be away and we'd have a final in the southern hemisphere." In terms of managing budgets and making provisional bookings for flights, it seems to have a practical purpose, but experienced Davis Cup watchers know that as soon as you get into such permutations, a shock result happens and all the provisional bookings go up in smoke.

Going into the 2006 quarterfinals, the safest bet seemed to be that Croatia would be in the semifinals – after all, Croatia was at home to Argentina, the nation that seemed unusually vulnerable to away ties. A victory would most likely take Croatia to Australia, and if the Australians won that, they would most likely play host to the USA in the final, as the Americans would probably have a winnable home semifinal against France.

Stringing together the permutations, the chances of a Melbourne final seemed considerable. But then the unexpected duly happened – and it was nothing to do with the Aussies. ●

CROATIA v **ARGENTINA**

IT WAS AS IF LOGIC HAD BEEN SUSPENDED AND MARIO ANCIC didn't quite know what to do. The Croat who had won the match that gave Croatia the 2005 Davis Cup by BNP Paribas sat stiffly in his chair at the post-draw news conference, explaining: "The doctors tell me I need seven days, but I don't have seven days." The implication was clear. Did the doctors not understand? This was Davis Cup! What did they mean, it takes seven days?

This was supposed to be the triumphant homecoming. The Croatian team had been given a rapturous welcome in Split in December 2005 when it returned victorious from the final in Bratislava, but this was the first home tie since that triumph, and in the country's capital, too. Now a freak accident was threatening to turn the celebration into a nightmare.

After practicing in late afternoon on the Wednesday, Ancic was warming down with some stretching exercises on a bench by the court. He had had some back problems in the past, but they were thought to belong there: in the past. Yet as he got up, his back seized up. "I almost fell to the ground," he said. "For the first ten minutes, I couldn't walk properly. It's a herniated disc, and this kind of injury takes time, but I don't have time."

To those who scoff at two-man Davis Cup teams, perhaps Croatia's predicament seemed poetic justice for a nation heavily dependent on two players. But it shouldn't have been so. Though Ancic and Ivan Ljubicic played all Croatia's live matches in 2005, there was a third member of the team, and a high-quality member: Ivo Karlovic. After all the waiting in the wings, this was surely Karlovic's moment.

But Karlovic wasn't there. The reason why may one day emerge, but no one was admitting to it over the quarterfinal weekend or immediately after. All that was said was

that Ljubicic, Croatia's playing captain, hadn't picked him. No one was taken in by that as a complete explanation. Clearly there was a disagreement about something, and whether Ljubicic should have been more accommodating or Karlovic less stubborn, the upshot was that Croatia's top reserve wasn't around when he was needed most.

With Ljubicic arriving on Tuesday with an upset stomach and generally feeling the fatigue from his great run to the final in Miami, and ticket sales for the three days in Zagreb's Dom Sportova arena flagging after a rise in prices that put them beyond most Croats' budgets, everything that could go wrong for Croatia seemed to be doing just that.

Yet Argentina hardly seemed ideally equipped to take advantage. The South American nation, so powerful on clay, has not traveled well in recent years, and came to Zagreb with no obvious second singles player. The previous year, the Argentinians seemed to have banished their poor away-record with a superb victory over Australia on the grass of Sydney, but that weekend was a personal triumph for David Nalbandian, who won his three matches. When Argentina traveled to Bratislava in the semifinals, the reliance on Nalbandian proved too much, Slovakia winning largely on the basis of taking the doubles. Since that semifinal, Argentina's second singles player, Guillermo Coria, had slumped in form, and the former French Open champion Gaston Gaudio seemed half-hearted about committing to national duty.

That left Argentina's captain, Alberto Mancini, having to rely on Argentina's tremendous strength in depth. With Jose Acasuso having done so well on his debut two months earlier, he kept his place, along with Agustin Calleri, who was picked primarily for the doubles, and the brooding Juan Ignacio Chela. Calleri's run to the quarterfinals in Miami, where he played well against Ljubicic, suddenly made him the obvious singles option, and he was nominated to play on the opening day.

Despite all their troubles, Croatia still had one ace in their hand: Ljubicic. Not just as a player, but as a captain. His two ties in 2006 as playing captain were always intended as a stop-gap arrangement, but what that quarterfinal weekend showed was that Ljubicic has all the qualities needed for being a superb Davis Cup captain at some stage in the future.

His first act was to nominate Ancic for the Friday. He knew Ancic had no chance of playing—he was fairly sure Ancic had no chance of playing at any stage in the weekend—but he didn't replace him so as to keep Argentina guessing, and to keep open the chance of a fitness miracle.

One could argue that nominating Ancic was against the spirit of the Davis Cup rules, which state that a player can only be replaced between the draw and one of the opening day's singles if certified as injured by an independent doctor. And it's a strong argument. But the wily Ljubicic was using a technicality to keep from Argentina whether he would play Sasa Tuksar or Marin Cilic in Ancic's place. By Wednesday night Cilic, the world's top-ranked junior at the time, knew he would be facing Nalbandian on Friday, but Argentina didn't know that until lunchtime on Friday.

And before Cilic got anywhere near the court, the weekend had had a dramatic start.

Ljubicic had arrived on the Tuesday from Miami. When Calleri took a two-set lead in the opening rubber, Ljubicic looked flat. The Croat then trailed 1–4 in another tiebreak in the third set. In an unusual admission for a home player, Ljubicic said later: "I was having

Pictured from top:

Agustin Calleri (ARG); Ivan Ljubicic (CRO);

David Nalbandian (ARG)

problems because it took me a long time to adapt to the court. I came late from Miami, hardly slept after having stomach problems, and practiced properly only on Thursday. I was just trying to hang on, win a set, and after that I knew that everything is possible. Early in the third set I looked at my watch—it was around four in the afternoon, ten in the morning Miami time, and I started to hit better."

One shot turned the match. With Calleri leading 4–1 in the tiebreak, Ljubicic attacked to his opponent's backhand and came to the net. Calleri had the chance of a pass but missed it. That was the let-off Ljubicic needed. He won the next four points, and though Calleri leveled the set at 6–6 to stand just two points from victory, the momentum had turned.

Not only did Ljubicic win the next two points to claim the tiebreak, but he won the next 15, too, going on to lead 5–0 in the fourth set. Calleri was a broken man, and won only three more games as Ljubicic ran out a 6–7(7) 5–7 7–6(6) 6–1 6–2 winner after four hours.

If that only enhanced Ljubicic's reputation as one of the Davis Cup's great players—it was his thirty-fourth win in the competition, taking him ahead of Ivanisevic—Nalbandian did the same for his own reputation in the second singles. Facing Cilic, he gave the teenager a lesson in the gulf that exists between the top five in juniors and the top five on the full tour. Cilic looked out of his depth, as Nalbandian conceded just four games in a ninety-one-minute demolition.

On Friday night, Ljubicic continued to play mind games, saying he would wait until the last minute before deciding whether to risk Ancic in the doubles. Ancic, predictably, was not fit, so Cilic came in to partner Ljubicic, while Calleri had expended so much energy that he made way for Acasuso, an experienced doubles player but who had never played with Nalbandian. Acasuso proved the man of the match in a 6–4 6–2 3–6 6–4 victory which continued a remarkable run for Argentina – it had won every doubles when fielding a new pairing since returning to the World Group in 2002.

The tie was now out of Ljubicic's hands, but that didn't stop him from delivering a masterclass against Nalbandian in the fourth rubber to set up a decisive match. The Croat hit thirty-five aces in his 6–3 6–4 6–4 victory, which gave him ten consecutive Davis Cup singles victories on home soil and earned him the admiration of even the most ardent Argentinian fans.

He did one other thing, which showed that, even at the height of combat against a fellow top-five player, he was still thinking as a captain. The match had begun with Ancic sitting in the captain's seat, and Croatia's fourth player, Tuksar, waiting in the locker room. Early in the third set, Ljubicic sent Ancic to the locker room and told Tuksar to sit in the stadium. The aim was to sow the seed of doubt in the visitors' minds—would Ancic be playing after all? Maybe he was fit?

He wasn't, and was never going to be. But the switch had something of an effect. Argentina's captain Mancini had decided the night before that Chela would contest the fifth rubber if it were live, and he faced Tuksar, a player in his first live Davis Cup rubber, in his first best-of-five-sets match, and having never previously played more than three hours at a stretch. But Tuksar was no respecter of reputations. Despite a ranking of 156 compared with Chela's 31, Tuksar stormed out to take the first set. Up to 4–4 in the second he played the match of his life, but then he got a little tight, and crucially lost his deadly first serve.

Pictured from top:

Marin Cilic (CRO), left, and Ivan Ljubicic (CRO); Argentinian fans; Playing captain Ivan Ljubicic (CRO), left, and Sasa Tuksar (CRO)

Pictured from top:

Wayne Arthurs (AUS), left, and Paul Hanley (AUS);

Max Mirnyi (BLR)

Pictured opposite:

Lleyton Hewitt (AUS)

CROATIA v **ARGENTINA** CONTINUED

As the nerves took over, the two men began playing long baseline rallies on one of the fastest courts permitted in tennis. Tuksar led the third set tiebreak 3–0 and 6–5, but Chela took the set. Yet the nerves were also affecting him. As Chela served for the tie at 5–4, he suddenly began to cramp, and took an injury timeout. After treatment to both legs, he came back, earned a match point, but blew it as Tuksar held on. Two more match points came and went at 6–5. Eventually Chela sealed Argentina's place in the semifinals on his fifth match point, a Tuksar forehand landing in the net. Argentina had done it, the 3–6 6–4 7–6(6) 7–6(5) victory in four hours twenty-one minutes representing Chela's greatest-ever Davis Cup win.

The champions were out, thanks to a mixture of bad luck and a little bad management. It could have been Karlovic's greatest moment—instead it was Chela's, as Argentina took another step toward ridding itself of its reputation as a poor away team. ●

AUSTRALIA v BELARUS

AS WELL AS TAKING TENNIS TO VENUES THE REGULAR TOUR CANNOT REACH, the Davis Cup by BNP Paribas also has the capacity to take top-level tennis back to the sport's traditional venues, some of which have been largely left behind by the onward march of commercial and technological progress. Hence the great delight among many of the sport's connoisseurs when Tennis Australia chose the Kooyong Club for its quarterfinal against Belarus.

The stadium that hosted the Australian national championships in rotation with four other venues from 1927 to 1970, and then had exclusive hosting rights to the Australian Open from 1971 to 1987, seems a relic of a bygone era. The beautiful club on the southeastern outskirts of the Melbourne conurbation has two long rows of grass courts, with the horseshoe-shaped main stadium nestling in a corner of Glenferrie Road and the elevated Monash Freeway. Next to the stadium is the clubhouse, kitted out with bars, a restaurant, and half a dozen squash courts. But there's nothing else—in fact, the complete lack of back-up infrastructure makes it seem strange that this venue had hosted a Grand Slam tennis tournament less than twenty years earlier.

Kooyong is a grass court club, and the main arena was built to have two courts side by side in the early stages of the tournament, then reverting to a single court in the relatively untouched center, so the matches in the climax to the championships were played on grass that hadn't had nearly a fortnight's wear and tear. These days a Rebound Ace court sits in the middle of the arena, used primarily for the exhibition tournament staged at Kooyong in the week before the Australian Open. All that remains of the original playing surface are two neat verges on either side of the aquamarine green of the rubberized hard court. But however "olde worlde" it may seem in the context of today's tennis tour, Kooyong has an ambience that still contains the magic of the greats who graced its lawns throughout the twentieth century.

And that ambience clearly got to Wayne Arthurs. The lefthander lives in Melbourne, is a member at the Kooyong Club, and was returning to competitive action for the first time

Pictured from top:

Vladimir Voltchkov (BLR); Chris Guccione (AUS);

Max Mirnyi (BLR), left, and Vladimir Voltchkov (BLR)

since the birth of his daughter, Amber, four weeks earlier. By now thirty-five, he was planning retirement in 2006, and the emotional experience of playing in the spiritual home of Australian tennis got to him. Had it not been for an inspired display by his doubles partner Paul Hanley, Australia may well have found itself going into the final day of the tie with at least one live match.

But in truth, the quarterfinal was killed off the moment Chris Guccione recorded his second superb Davis Cup performance in two months in the opening rubber. Although Australia were favorites, the absence of an obvious second singles player for the home nation meant Belarus had a chance, if Max Mirnyi and Vladimir Voltchkov could each beat Australia's No. 2 and they could sneak the doubles. That plan disappeared with Guccione's 7–6(4) 3–6 7–5 3–6 6–4 win over Mirnyi, and by Saturday night Australia's main interest was who would win in Zagreb between Croatia—who Australia would have hosted in the semifinals—and Argentina, which meant a trip to Buenos Aires.

Guccione described it as "the biggest win of my life." In time, he will probably see it as a slightly lesser achievement than his win over George Bastl in Geneva two months earlier. Then he was playing a live fifth rubber away from home—this time it was a first rubber, at home, and one he was expected to lose, but the presence of the Melburnian's friends and family probably made it more personally satisfying for him.

He was certainly satisfied with the way he turned a 1–4 deficit in the first set tiebreak into a 7–4 success. And the way he bounced back to break in the eleventh game of the third set, after being broken when he served for a 2–1 lead in the previous game, showed maturity beyond his twenty years. Both players had breaks midway through the fifth set, but at 4–5 Mirnyi faltered and a missed volley meant Guccione had given Australia the vital point of the weekend.

"Sure we're a little disappointed," a philosophical Mirnyi told the Australian media. "You guys are so happy, Chris Guccione is a new hero—isn't that what Davis Cup is all about?"

Voltchkov has done his fair share of showing what Davis Cup is all about, but with Mirnyi having lost in five sets, the wind was out of Voltchkov's sails. And that's just the time you don't want to be playing Lleyton Hewitt clad in Australia's green and gold. The former world No. 1 needed just ninety-two minutes to see Australia into a 2–0 lead, conceding five games in gusty conditions to win 6–2 6–1 6–2. "He pretty much played as well as he can," said Voltchkov. "I think it was just difficult today, it was like hitting against a wall, and as a child I learned you would never beat the wall."

Though the game was effectively up for Belarus, Mirnyi and Voltchkov put up a spirited showing in the doubles. But the day turned into a triumph for Arthurs and Hanley, for different reasons. For Arthurs it was a win at his home club in probably his final year on the tour. For Hanley it was the kind of statesmanlike performance that some prominent Australian tennis observers once thought him incapable of delivering.

A pivotal moment came when Hanley accidentally hit a ball that struck Arthurs on the back of the head. That not only woke up the veteran, but reminded him of the doubles in the 2003 final, when he and Todd Woodbridge outclassed Spain's Alex Corretja and Feliciano Lopez, dropping just three games as Australia won its twenty-eighth Davis Cup. In that match, Arthurs hit Woodbridge on the head with a ball, and from the moment Hanley had returned the favor, Arthurs found himself thinking back to the 2003 final at Melbourne Park—and getting inspired by it.

The visitors had their chances in the Aussies' 3–6 6–4 5–7 6–3 7–5 win, but the tide was with Australia, who went on to win the two dead rubbers for a 5–0 scoreline. The result kept intact an unbeaten streak for Australia at Kooyong. Built in 1926, it hosted its first Davis Cup tie twenty years later in the 1946 final, and the home nation has never lost there. It therefore seemed strange that it had been thirteen years since the previous tie at Kooyong— no doubt it will be less than another thirteen before the venerable oval-shaped stadium sees Davis Cup by BNP Paribas action again. ●

USA v CHILE

VICTORIA MCENROE WILL NO DOUBT ONE DAY KNOW THE FUSS she caused a full fortnight before she entered this world. As the daughter of the U.S. Davis Cup captain Patrick McEnroe practiced her footwork in her mother Melissa's womb, her dad had to relinquish control—at least temporarily—of the team he had nurtured over the previous five years. At his home in Manhattan, he watched on television as his charges battled against Chile in the California desert. But however the story is one day told to Ms. McEnroe Jr, it ought to include the good that came out of it.

That good was the public confirmation that Andy Roddick and Dean Goldfine really are friends first and ex-business associates second. Goldfine had missed his first Davis Cup tie for three years in the first round, as Roddick had ended their thirteen-month coaching relationship just a few days earlier. But when Victoria's birth looked like it might clash with the USA-Chile Davis Cup by BNP Paribas quarterfinal, Roddick was as vociferous as his teammates in calling for Goldfine to fill McEnroe's shoes.

"No matter what's gone on in business, we're good friends," said Roddick of his relationship with Goldfine. Many a tennis player has said something similar and meant, well, something a little less cordial (one might even include Roddick in that group), but there was no doubt Roddick meant it this time. Goldfine clearly enjoyed his moment. In one press conference when he was giving a well-thought-out answer, Roddick chastised him for taking so long. "Hey, this is my one time as captain," Goldfine retorted, all in great spirit.

More important, the weekend proved Roddick's coming-out party for 2006. The top American (at the time) was, by his own high standards, stagnating. A semifinal in San Jose and a quarterfinal in Miami were the best the former No. 1 had to show since his fourth round exit to Marcos Baghdatis at the Australian Open, his last event working with Goldfine. By the time Roddick walked out onto the lush lawns of the Mission Hills Country Club, he was facing a real test of character.

Mission Hills is a gated residential community in Rancho Mirage, a small settlement in the California desert. When it became clear the USA would be playing Chile, Roddick made a strong play for grass, and in the few weeks available to organize the tie, Mission Hills seemed the only grass court venue that could be prepared in time. It worked well for the club, and the courts were in good shape.

Pictured from top:

U.S. team press conference; Fernando Gonzalez (CHI)

USA v CHILE CONTINUED

But they had been chosen for Roddick, whereas America's second player, James Blake, had posted most of his good results on hard courts. And on the first day, Blake was up against a Chilean, Fernando Gonzalez, who had proved his grass court credentials the previous year.

Ah yes, the Chileans. To most observers, the visitors were almost overlooked. This was the Americans' tie, wasn't it? Roddick and Blake were both in the world's top ten; Gonzalez and Nicolas Massu were a two-man team who had to play on all three days; the visiting nation was being dragged screaming off its favorite clay and onto the surface it liked least—the result seemed a foregone conclusion.

Yet the Chileans came to Rancho Mirage with a great attitude. They didn't see themselves as cannon fodder; their captain, Hans Gildemeister, talked and acted as if his team, though underdogs, had every chance of winning; and the Chilean players had the memories of some great performances against the Americans at the Athens Olympics. Whatever the spectators may have felt, no way were the American players going to underestimate their opponents.

After two sets of the opening match, all the favors were for the home side, as Blake led 7–6 6–0, and Gonzalez had to have treatment for an upper back problem. But in the tenth game of the third set, the tide turned. Serving for the match at 30–15, Blake thought he'd won the point when the line umpire called a Gonzalez backhand out. But the umpire Pascal Maria overruled and ordered the point to be replayed. Gonzalez seized his chance, broke Blake, and once he'd taken the set on a tiebreak, he was into the match.

With the few hundred Chilean fans making more noise than the few thousand Americans, the USA's home advantage seemed to have dwindled. And Blake had never won a five-set match—he went into this one having lost all his six, his previous two from two-sets up. So when Gonzalez took the fourth set 6–4, the Chilean became the favorite, and a break in the seventeenth game of the decider followed by four aces gave him a 6–7(5) 0–6 7–6(2) 6–4 10–8 win.

Blake was characteristically statesmanlike after the match. "I think it's been blown out of proportion that the grass was meant to make them uncomfortable," he said. "It was all about our being comfortable. It's the surface Andy is most comfortable on and I think he's the second-best grass court player in the world. This was a decision made for the good of our team."

But that put the onus on Roddick to make good the damage. The world's fastest server had amassed plenty of experience in picking up the pieces after an opening defeat, and Blake had bailed him out in the first round after Roddick had lost to Andrei Pavel, so Roddick was keen to show that team cooperation worked both ways. This was his moment.

"I was just excited that I could cover James's back today, like he had mine in La Jolla," Roddick said after his impressive 6–3 7–6(5) 7–6(5) win. "When he went down, I really wanted to go out there and get it for him. He covered my butt in La Jolla and really saved the tie."

Though he wasn't to know it until Saturday morning, Blake had performed a great service for the USA. The four hours, twenty minutes he had kept Gonzalez on court left the Chileans in a dilemma—there was no doubt Gonzalez and Massú were good enough to beat

Pictured from top:

Nicolas Massu (CHI); James Blake (USA);

Paul Capdeville (CHI), left, and Adrian Garcia (CHI)

Pictured opposite:

Andy Roddick (USA)

Pictured from top:
Bob and Mike Bryan (USA); Mission Hills Country Club

Bob and Mike Bryan, but how much would it take out of them? Even if they won, would that leave them drained for the reverse singles?

In the end, Gildemeister opted to throw the doubles. That wasn't the vocabulary he used, but against the best pair in the world, Chile's second-string team of Adrian Garcia and Paul Capdeville barely stood a chance, and Bob Bryan used the match for his own personal tour de force. The lefthander of the twins didn't drop a point on his own serve until the eighth game he served, by which time the USA had match point. That one was saved by a Garcia backhand to put a blotch on Bob's record, but after the next point, the Americans led 2–1 thanks to a 6–1 6–2 6–4 win in barely an hour.

Yet Gildemeister's gamble seemed to be paying off as Gonzalez took the first set of the reverse singles against Roddick. For much of the second set the Chilean's fighting spirit seemed set to carry him to victory, but Roddick had never lost a match when playing to give his team the tie, and when he broke in the twelfth game of the second set, a seventh decisive victory was suddenly back on the agenda.

The match really turned in the eighth game of the third set, when Gonzalez suffered two dubious line calls. When Roddick broke and then held serve for a two-sets-to-one lead, Gonzalez smashed his racket in anger. The reaction was indicative of the way the wind had changed direction, and two breaks in the fourth set gave Roddick the match, 4–6 7–5 6–3 6–2.

The USA had reached the semifinals with wins on a hard court in La Jolla and on grass in Rancho Mirage. But results elsewhere meant there could be no more home ties in 2006 for the thirty-one-time champions. After the sunshine of California, the next step on the journey would be the indoor clay of Moscow. ●

FRANCE v **RUSSIA**

SOME PEOPLE DIDN'T RECOGNIZE HIM. He had only played three tournaments since Wimbledon, and in that time his hair had grown untamed in a way that revealed its full curly splendor. As it had always been fairly short, the effect gave him a degree of short-term anonymity, which he seemed to be enjoying.

Marat Safin was back. The unpredictable Muscovite, whose awesome power belied a body that frequently proved insufficiently robust to withstand the relentless rigors of the global tennis tour, was returning to the Davis Cup fold for the first time in thirteen months, after missing Russia's 2005 quarterfinal and semifinal with a condition known as "jumper's knee." The injury had caused him to miss seven months of competitive action, and his return had been the usual mix of the brilliant and the baffling. Now in just his fourth event back, few knew what to expect.

Would he play singles? Would he only play doubles? A fully fit Safin might have been expected to play on all three days, as Russia's most feared singles player and in a partnership with Mikhail Youzhny that seemed to represent Russia's best doubles option. As he sat at the draw, the bored look on his face partially hidden by a few stray ringlets and several days' growth of beard, it became clear that Russia's captain, Shamil Tarpischev, was gambling on Safin the singles player.

In one sense it was an appropriate tie for Safin's return to the team competition. The first tie his troublesome knee had caused him to miss was also against France: the 2005 quarterfinal played on an indoor clay court in Moscow. Now, Russia was drawn to play France for the third time in five years—one of the refrains of the weekend was, "It wouldn't be Davis Cup without France playing Russia!"—but this time, France had a somewhat stronger team than the one that narrowly lost in 2005. Richard Gasquet, a debutant in Moscow, had added the experience of the 2006 first round tie against Germany and looked a better player than nine months earlier, and France's most experienced team member, Sebastien Grosjean, was back after a 2005 characterized by several absences.

But the French were struck a blow early in the week. Grosjean hurt his back, and while it was improving day by day, it was clear by Wednesday that he wouldn't be ready to play one of the opening singles matches. Although Arnaud Clement had improved his singles ranking and was back on the verge of the top 50, he was a clear underdog against the sixth-ranked Nikolay Davydenko.

That meant Gasquet was under pressure to beat Safin in the opening rubber. After an hour, it looked bad for the French, despite the vociferous support of the sports-mad public of Pau. Safin was a set up, and playing a level of tennis that at times was outstanding.

But Gasquet is passionate about playing for his country. Brought up with France's triumphs, the Davis Cup by BNP Paribas means so much to him, and in a corner of France that is not far from where Gasquet grew up, he was determined to get back. An early break in the second set was just enough to level the match, but Safin bounced back to take the third. The Russian looked good to take the match in four sets, but a superb tiebreak by Gasquet took it into a final set.

If not a great match, it was certainly a very good one, and it looked like it would be decided on who had greater reserves of strength. Safin, still short of match practice, broke in the second game, and suddenly Gasquet seemed tired. A second break allowed Safin to win 7-6(4) 4-6 6-3 6-7(1) 6-1 in three hours and forty-two minutes of enthralling tennis. "It was the best win since my comeback," he said, "in fact it was my best win since I won the Australian Open."

In some people's eyes it was the decisive point of the weekend, but there was a lot more tennis left, and the outcome was in doubt until well into Sunday afternoon.

Clement came remarkably close to beating Davydenko in the second singles. After a great start that gave the Frenchman the first set, Davydenko gradually got into the match, taking the second and third sets, and opening up a 4-1 lead in the fourth. But the Russian was using up a lot of nervous energy, and when Clement broke back, things suddenly became very tense. Clement took the set into the tiebreak, and as he prepared to play the opening point, Davydenko winced when flexing his hip and thigh. He won the first three points, but when he made uncharacteristic errors on the fourth and fifth to lead just 3-2, it was clear he was in trouble and called for the trainer.

Whether it's right that a player can have massage mid-tiebreak is a source of constant debate in the tennis world—it seems so unfair to the uninjured player. But it is allowed, so Davydenko—an intrinsically fair competitor—was not breaching any rules in having both his thighs massaged. The pause broke Clement's rhythm, and Davydenko went on to take the

Pictured from top:

Marat Safin (RUS); Arnaud Clement (FRA);
Pau's Palais des Sports

tiebreak 7–4 to give him a 3–6 6–2 6–4 7–6(4) win and Russia a 2–0 lead after the first day.

"I knew my last chance to win the match was in that tiebreak," Davydenko said afterward. "If he had won the fourth set, I would have had to retire in the fifth." The Russian had in fact damaged his thigh and couldn't play on the final day. Clement had come agonizingly close to leveling the tie.

And what a difference that might have made. With news from the French camp suggesting Grosjean would be fit to face Safin in the fifth rubber, a French win in the doubles would leave the tie very open. After playing five sets and possibly needing to play five more on Sunday, Safin was wisely rested on the Saturday, Russia fielding the scratch pairing of Youzhny and Dmitry Tursunov against the experienced French team of Clément and Michael Llodra. In a superb display of teamwork that left the Russians looking out of their depth, the French took the opening two sets. But when they missed three break points at 3–3 in the third, the momentum turned Russia's way. At 2–2 in the fifth, the visitors looked well set to seal their semifinal place in two days, but suddenly the French pair rediscovered their form of the first two-and-a-half sets, and ran out 6–3 6–3 6–7(3) 5–7 6–2 winners.

When the news came through an hour before play on Sunday that Davydenko had been replaced by Tursunov, it was impossible to say who was now favored to win. It was Tursunov's debut in a live Davis Cup singles rubber, but his form was impressive, and he is one of the strongest players on the tour. That strength was to prove crucial.

After an appalling start that raised questions about his physical endurance, Gasquet got into the match in the second set, and many people thought he had won the third when he had set point at 5–4. A Tursunov backhand was seen by many to be out, but not by the line judge—yet a ball boy reacted to the crowd, ran onto the court, and the point had to be replayed. Tursunov saved the set point with a service winner, and went on to lead 4–2 in the tiebreak, but the Russian then suffered a bad call, and made five unforced errors as Gasquet took a two-sets-to-one lead.

Tursunov bounced back to take an early break in the fourth, and as the fifth set wore on, both players were running on their reserve tanks. Gasquet threw everything at Tursunov, who was beginning to play more controlled tennis than his usual big-hitting style. At 5–5, Tursunov earned a break point, and the most dramatic point of the match ended with Gasquet flat on his back and the indefatigable Tursunov serving for the match. After all the effort, the Russian wasn't going to let his moment pass, and served out the victory to love.

Asked courtside by an interviewer how he felt, the laconic American-educated Russian said: "I dunno. Pretty darn happy, I guess." Gasquet had no regrets about the way he had played, saying of his opponent: "Today he was a monster."

In answer to all the questions about the number of times France had faced Russia in the Davis Cup, France's captain Guy Forget replied that he was not sick of facing the Russians, only sick of losing to them. Yet the Russians had beaten the French for the third time in five years and had broken the five-year sequence the French fans had been pinning their superstitious hopes on. France had won the cup in 1991, 1996, and 2001—2006 was the natural progression, but thanks to the combined strength of Safin, Davydenko, and Tursunov, it was not to be. ●

Pictured from top:

The doubles rubber; Nikolay Davydenko (RUS);

Marat Safin (RUS)

Pictured opposite from top:

Dmitry Tursunov (RUS); Richard Gasquet (FRA), left,

and captain Guy Forget

THE AGONY AND THE ECSTASY

Davis Cup brings out strong emotions, with the highs and the lows of the competition—and
sometimes a curious mixture of both—written on its players' faces.

Name
ANDY RODDICK

Born
BORN 30 AUGUST 1982 IN
OMAHA, NEBRASKA, USA

Turned professional
2000

If ever there was a question mark about Andy Roddick's effectiveness as a Davis Cup player, it was answered emphatically over the quarterfinal weekend when the USA hosted Chile in Rancho Mirage, California.

PLAYER OF THE ROUND

RODDICK HAD ARRIVED STRUGGLING FOR FORM. He departed having delivered two performances that would have left any casual observer wondering what the talk of a crisis in his confidence was all about.

Roddick was suffering a minor crisis of confidence. He had slipped from third to fifth in the rankings and was about to slide still further. He had parted from his coach, Dean Goldfine, and his stock in the tennis world was falling. Yet he was putting in the work, and he knew it would click when the moment was right. That the Davis Cup by BNP Paribas should provide that moment was no surprise.

Roddick has been the mainstay of an American Davis Cup team who has had none of the reluctance to turn out that sometimes accompanied the USA's gold-plated generation of the 1990s. If Pete Sampras lost some interest because his heroics in the 1995 final cut too little ice back home, that has never been a problem for Roddick since he was given his debut in Patrick McEnroe's first tie as captain, an abortive mission to Switzerland in February 2001.

Talk of a relative lack of interest in America was around as Roddick prepared to face the nationalistically passionate Chileans, but Roddick was not letting it dampen his devotion to the cause. "This tie is obviously the biggest story down there [in Chile], he said. "I wish it was that way here, but as far as needing attention to feel an emotional lift for Davis Cup, I don't think our team needs that at all." And when asked about the format that required him to play a tie eight weeks after the first, he replied: "I'll play the format that I have. I have no other option right now. The only other option is not playing. In my mind, that's not an option. I love Davis Cup. I love competing for my country. There are no other options in my mind."

There was one other factor that perhaps lifted Roddick to being the Davis Cup player of the quarterfinal weekend. In his junior days he played tennis against Drew Brees, who went on to become a celebrated quarterback in American football. Three months before the quarterfinal tie, Brees needed arthroscopic surgery on a badly injured shoulder. While out of competition, he sought out his old buddy from junior days, and the two stars chatted about the rough and tumble of a top-level athlete's life.

Spurred on by that and by his team, Roddick dismissed a characteristically never-say-die challenge from Nicolas Massu to steady the U.S. ship after James Blake had lost a marathon five-setter to Fernando Gonzalez. And playing to take his country into the semifinals, Roddick absorbed the battering of a set and a half of Gonzalez's best tennis before turning the match around, thanks in part to some diving volleys on crucial points midway through the second set.

"This has definitely been the best weekend for me so far," Roddick said after his four-set win over Gonzalez. "I've kind of been looking for something good, maybe this was it. I came up pretty big this weekend, especially today."

Roddick's status as a team player is so high that even his closest buddies can joke about him. At the team's pre-draw press conference three days before the quarterfinal began, Blake allowed himself the jocular remark "No one likes Andy." "You know they're going to write that," said Roddick, pointing to the press. "Of course they are," said Blake. Needless to say no one did write it, because there wasn't a shred of truth in it—and everyone present knew it. ●

semifinals 22-24 SEPTEMBER

Argentina defeated Australia 5–0   BUENOS AIRES, ARGENTINA—OUTDOOR CLAY

Russia defeated USA 3–2   MOSCOW, RUSSIA—INDOOR CLAY

SEMIFINALS

ONCE THE QUARTERFINALS HAD PRODUCED THE SEMIFINAL LINEUP, the final seemed obvious: it had to be Russia against Argentina. After all, the Australians didn't seem to have a chance playing away to Argentina, and Russia was thought to be too strong against an American team still vulnerable on clay.

Ultimately, that's how it turned out, but in the five months between the quarters and the semis, the sands of the tennis world shifted to a significant extent. In April, Russia's Igor Andreev underwent complex surgery on his left knee that would force him to miss the Americans' visit to Moscow. In May, James Blake won a handful of matches on red clay, to suggest that he could play on the surface. In July, Mark Philippoussis returned to the tour and won the title in Newport, Rhode Island. In early September, Lleyton Hewitt decided he would make the trip to Buenos Aires after all. And all this time, Argentina's golden age was taking something of a pit stop, with only David Nalbandian's run to the semifinals in Paris a result of significance for the powerful nation at either the French Open or Wimbledon.

As the four teams assembled in opposing hemispheres, suddenly the outcome of the two ties didn't seem quite such a foregone conclusion after all. ●

RUSSIA v USA

AN INSPIRED BIT OF CAPTAINCY OR SOME ADEPT CRISIS MANAGEMENT? That was the question hanging in the air after Russia reached its second final in four years in arguably the greatest set of tennis seen in the 2006 Davis Cup by BNP Paribas World Group. Yet that set, won 17–15 by Dmitry Tursunov over Andy Roddick, was itself the product of some behind-the-scenes turmoil that the wily Russian captain Shamil Tarpischev turned gloriously to his nation's advantage.

There's a belief in the art world that great creativity comes from chaos, not order. It's not a belief common in sport——the motto of most top-level coaches is if you want to succeed, get your house in order. Yet there was certainly some disorder in the Russian camp in the run-up to the semifinals. First, there was Igor Andreev's unavailability, and Tursunov was happy telling people that his clay court record wouldn't have merited his selection if Andreev had been fit. Second, how fit was Marat Safin? The hero of the first day against France had posted a handful of wins in the intervening months, but had not put together a serious streak. Third, how prepared for the tie was Russia's top-ranked player, the world No. 5 Nikolay Davydenko?

In Andreev's absence, the squad of Davydenko, Safin, Tursunov, and Mikhail Youzhny had rather selected itself, with Davydenko expected to play two singles. But while Youzhny, Safin, and Tursunov had all concentrated on clay court preparation after the US Open, Davydenko had chosen to play the tour event in Beijing on hard court, and had retired in the quarterfinals citing dizziness.

So when Tarpischev nominated Safin and Youzhny to play the opening day's singles, several eyebrows were raised. Was the Russian captain exacting some quiet discipline on his wayward No. 1? Tarpischev is, after all, different from many—if not most—Davis Cup captains. He is not in situ by the grace of his players. He is one of the most influential men in Russia, he is a member of the International Olympic Committee, and he is Mr. Russian Tennis, being

president of the national association, as well as captain of the Davis Cup and Fed Cup teams. So there were many who wondered whether Davydenko's decision to pursue Tennis Masters Cup points—and no doubt a few dollars of appearance money—had angered his captain.

Ultimately, Tarpischev was just making the decision he felt was best for the team. He could see Davydenko was mentally tired, if not physically doubtful too. Youzhny had made it to the US Open semifinals and brought a good Davis Cup record to the table. "Davydenko has not yet reacclimatized after his trip to Beijing," Tarpischev said, "so I'm giving him an extra couple of days to be ready." As it happened, Davydenko took no active part in the weekend, a slight fever ruling him out of both Sunday's matches. It was not as healthy a Russian lineup as it looked.

Yet out of such disorder emerged a quite outstanding fourth rubber, which will forever remain to the credit of Tursunov and Roddick, whatever else they go on to achieve.

The frustrating element for Roddick was that he didn't discover his form and tactics of the third, fourth, and fifth sets of his 6–3 6–4 5–7 3–6 17–15 defeat two days earlier, or even two sets earlier. He came into the tie having rediscovered his confidence with a Masters Series title in Cincinnati and a run to the final of the US Open, where he took a set off the seemingly invincible Roger Federer. A central factor in Roddick's revival was that he had begun working with Jimmy Connors, who had got him to "get in the face of his opponents" more, much the way Connors had done in the 1970s and '80s. Yet those tactics were never going to work so well on a soft clay court, which called for great patience as it was regularly breaking up and needed constant repair work by the Olympic Stadium's ground staff.

Roddick had perhaps wanted to play well on the opening day just a little too much. He delivered an aggressive but ultimately rushed performance against Safin, who evoked memories of his best days in a 6–4 6–3 7–6(5) win. Only when the Russian served for the match at 5–3 in the third set did he wobble, allowing Roddick his sole break of the match. With Roddick leading 5–2 in the tiebreak, a fourth set looked likely, but the American was still too dependent on his first serve, and when he missed two first serves at 5–4 and 5–5, Safin was home.

Tursunov hadn't been expected to play more than the doubles rubber, and when he had something of a nightmare in Bob and Mike Bryan's 6–3 6–4 6–2 masterclass of a win over Tursunov and Youzhny, Tarpischev's choice for the task of facing Roddick in the fourth rubber appeared to be between Davydenko and Youzhny, Youzhny having put in a polished performance to beat James Blake 7–5 1–6 6–1 7–5 in the second rubber. But with Youzhny having played seven sets over the first two days, Tarpischev opted not for Davydenko, who had had a mild temperature on the Saturday night, but for the man who had won the decisive fourth rubber for Russia the round before. When news of Tursunov's selection circulated around the Olympic Stadium in the hour before the third day's play began, the instinctive reaction was to plan for a long evening, as Roddick was fully expected to take the tie into a live fifth rubber. Yet to have such a reaction is to misunderstand Tursunov.

The man who seems emotionless when speaking but whose sparkle and eccentric wit come out when he writes (as witnessed by a highly entertaining daily blog he wrote for the ATP's website while at the 2006 Estoril Open) delivered two-and-a-half sets of model clay court tennis. If Rafael Nadal had used the angles and well-timed drop shots as well as

Pictured from top:

James Blake (USA); Mikhail Youzhny (RUS)

Pictured from top:

Bob and Mike Bryan (USA); U.S. captain Patrick McEnroe;

Igor Andreev (RUS), left, and Dmitry Tursunov (RUS)

Pictured opposite:

Marat Safin (RUS)

Tursunov did, people would have been purring that this just showed the class of the French Open champion. Yet this was a man who thought he couldn't play on clay.

Such unexpected dominance brought Roddick to the brink of desperation—but it also woke him up. Knowing his opponent would soon have the pressure of having to finish the job, Roddick developed a patience sorely missing from his game against Safin and in the first two sets against Tursunov. He knew Tursunov would throw in a couple of bad service games—he just needed to be ready to take advantage.

The first bad game came at 5–6 and allowed Roddick to nick the third set. At 3-4 in the fourth, Tursunov again came under pressure, Roddick playing a series of controlled points as his opponent became a little tight, and a measured point ending in an elegant backhand volley allowed Roddick to break. Moments later, with the match clock showing two hours thirty-three minutes, the two men were level.

At that point Roddick looked the stronger. He had been bludgeoned into finding the right strategy for clay, and having dented Tursunov's confidence, the fifth set seemed his for the taking. Yet Tursunov gave nothing away at the start of the set, and at 5-4 he had Roddick at 0–30. On any other surface Roddick would have relied on his big serve—but on clay he needed the full range of his game. All parts—including patience—served him well, and he leveled at 5–5. When Roddick then broke for 6–5, he stood on the verge of the kind of win that would have set him up for the rest of his career. But on the point of victory, he made two bad errors, and Tursunov broke back to 30.

Five more times Roddick served to stay in the match, and five more he held. But at 11–12, Tursunov stood at 15–40 with two match points. Again, all the constituent parts of Roddick's game came together to save those two plus a third match point. When Roddick held for 12–12, the momentum seemed back in his favor. Twice he brought Tursunov back from 40-0 to deuce, as both men played as economically as possible to conserve dwindling energy, but he couldn't make the breakthrough.

When Roddick held serve for 15–15, it was clear the two men would at least equal the longest-ever final set for a singles match in Davis Cup World Group history (the 17–15 with which Germany's Michael Westphal beat Tomas Smid of Czechoslovakia in the 1985 semifinals). They seemed likely to beat it, but with Roddick serving for the eleventh time to stay in the match, Tursunov struck. At 30–30, Roddick netted a tired backhand to give Tursunov a fourth match point. At 30–40, Roddick's approach shot sat up, he committed to his backhand wing a fraction too early, and that allowed Tursunov to stroke the ball gently down the line to end the two-and-a-quarter-hour set and send Russia into the final.

It was a dramatic and glorious end to a weekend that had taken three days to reach the boil, but there's no doubt the Russians were the worthy winners. For in Tursunov's victory, the home side had proved it could play well on any surface, while the visitors were shown up to be still vulnerable on clay.

Perhaps the key to the Tursunov-Roddick match was that Tursunov's emotions are forever under control. "I was on a 5 a.m. flight the next morning," he recalled two weeks later, "and by the time I was on the plane I had forgotten about the match, I had moved on." He moved on to win his first tour title the following week in Mumbai, remarking: "It's hard to get nervous after matches like that [against Roddick]."

"I feel like I let my team down," said Roddick half an hour after losing to Tursunov, "because it means we won't win the Davis Cup for another year." That was the sad side to this semifinal. The American team ethic built by Patrick McEnroe seemed to merit a Davis Cup triumph but, despite the outstanding contribution of the Bryans, the esprit de corps was unable to make up for the vulnerability on red clay of Roddick and Blake. ●

ARGENTINA v AUSTRALIA

TO SAY THIS TIE WAS A TRIUMPH—OR EVEN A DOUBLE TRIUMPH—FOR ARGENTINA sounds like simple sporting cliche. Yet however much some sections of the media make modest victories sound like earth-shattering events and thus devalue the currency of superlatives, this was without question a momentous weekend in the history of Argentinian tennis.

The first triumph was the simple one of Argentina reaching only its second final in the 107–year history of the competition. "In the first hours you don't realize what you have achieved but in the following days you see the real importance of it," said Argentina's captain, Alberto Mancini, after his team had sealed victory over Australia. And through tears of joy, he added: "To beat Australia here at home in the semifinals, it's something special. We are very emotional people as you can see and that's why I am overwhelmed."

The second triumph was perhaps the one of greater long-term significance. There's no question the first decade of the twenty-first century will go down as a golden era for Argentinian tennis, but golden ages eventually disappear, leaving behind them albums of memories, but not always a significant legacy. Yet the 2006 Davis Cup by BNP Paribas semifinal marked the moment when a significant part of the legacy of Argentina's golden tennis era was secured.

Despite the boom that accompanied the successes of Guillermo Vilas and Jose-Luis Clerc in the 1970s and early '80s, the nerve center of Argentina's tennis community had remained the Buenos Aires Lawn Tennis Club. It hosted most of the country's Davis Cup ties despite having a main stadium with a seating capacity of just 6,000, which for a large tie was proving increasingly limited. A temporary stadium holding 10,300 in the Parque Julio Roca was erected for the 2006 first round tie against Sweden (see page 39), with hints that if Argentina had a big home semifinal, the stadium would be made permanent as the first step toward an Argentinian national tennis center, complete with training complex and administrative accommodation.

Such hinted promises have the potential to evaporate, but following Juan Ignacio Chela's win over Sasa Tuksar in the quarterfinals, Argentina had its big home semifinal against the twenty-eight-time former champions, Australia. And thanks to a deal between the city authorities, the Argentina tennis association, and private business, a magnificent 14,000-seater stadium was built for the Argentina-Australia semifinal in the Parque Roca. To some, the magnificence of a purpose-built tennis stadium—which will eventually have a roof—just a couple of kilometers from some of the poorest urban areas of South America may seem somewhat incongruous; on the other hand, one could argue it brings tennis to a wider social cross-section than keeping it in the affluent confines of the Belgrano suburb that houses the Buenos Aires LTC. Either way, the Parque Roca on the south side of Buenos Aires can now be

Pictured from top:
Mark Philippoussis (AUS); the Parque Roca, Buenos Aires; David Nalbandian (ARG)
Pictured opposite from top:
Andy Roddick (USA); Boris Yeltsin, left, and Dmitry Tursunov (RUS)

ARGENTINA v AUSTRALIA CONTINUED

considered the new center of tennis in Argentina, and when finished, it will be the legacy of the generation of Nalbandian, Gaudio, Coria, et al.

It would have been fitting if the first tie to be played in the permanent stadium had been a celebration of glorious weather, brilliant tennis, and great sportsmanship. To be honest, it wasn't—there had been too much tactical sniping and settling of old scores in the lead-up to the semifinal for great sportsmanship to take center stage, and the weather was mixed. But as Australia's captain, John Fitzgerald, was right to admit, Argentina was simply the better team over the weekend.

Australia came to Buenos Aires with a vastly better lineup than the one that lost 5–0 in February 2002, when Lleyton Hewitt was recovering from chickenpox. Yet since that tie Hewitt's relationship with Argentina's players had deteriorated significantly. Comments he made hinting at a link between a spate of independent positive doping tests among Argentinian players hardly endeared him to the South American nation, though it added to the Argentinians' joy when they beat Australia on grass in Sydney in the 2005 quarterfinals.

With Australia due to travel to Buenos Aires for the 2006 semifinal, Argentina's top player and Davis Cup talisman David Nalbandian seemed to be heightening the tension. Whether it was a calculated gamble to dissuade Australia's best player from traveling to Buenos Aires or a genuine expression of loathing, it created a tetchy few days leading up to the tie. Whatever other personal off-court battles Hewitt was fighting that week, the Australian at least seemed to be doing what he could to build bridges with the Argentinian public, making a number of appeasing comments in Australia's pre- and post-draw press conferences.

Perhaps that helped contribute to an atmosphere that was raucously partisan—"wall-to-wall noise" was how Fitzgerald described it—but not really intimidating in an unfair manner. There were indeed shouts and whistles during Australian players' ball tosses, missed first serves were cheered, and at one stage a scream from the crowd caused a point to be replayed. But the tie's referee, Stefan Fransson, never had to invoke the "partisan crowd" rule, and even the most illustrious spectator at the tie, Argentina's former football idol Diego Maradona, had modified his support from the first round tie against Sweden, opting to cheer his own team rather than hurl insults at the visitors.

Hewitt knew that his chances of keeping the crowd out of the tie lay with his keeping Australia in the running. His match against Jose Acasuso on the opening day was always going to be the crucial rubber—if Hewitt lost, Argentina would be home and dry; but if he won, Australia would at least have a fighting chance.

That was because the Aussie team was much more impressive than many had expected. The former Wimbledon and US Open runner-up Mark Philippoussis had returned from injury to win the tour title in Newport in July, and while he was no longer the force that had helped Australia to the Davis Cup titles of 1999 and 2003, he seemed good enough to win a fifth rubber if the tie had come to it. His 6–4 6–3 6–3 defeat to Nalbandian in the opening match was a creditable showing, even if the outcome was never in doubt after Nalbandian had broken in the seventh game.

But for a fifth rubber to be at all plausible, Hewitt had to beat Acasuso. After three sets things were going well for the Australian, and when he had a break point in the fifth game of the fourth, he was minimizing the crowd as a factor. But having planted the seed of doubt

among the home fans, Hewitt needed to see it grow. He didn't. He missed his break point, and when Acasuso held serve for 3–2, the crowd found its full voice.

Hewitt was suddenly up against an opponent on his favorite surface, being urged on by 13,500 unleashed supporters. Acasuso surged to a run of eight games, which turned the perilous 2–2 situation in the fourth set into a 4–0 lead in the fifth. The dark clouds were gathering for Australia—both metaphorically and literally.

Hewitt needed three breaks to pull the match out of Acasuso's bag. He worked his way to break point at 0–4, when the heavens opened. And did they open! Torrential rain fell amid thunder and lightning, causing play to be abandoned for the day barely half an hour after the players had left the court.

When Hewitt took the first point after the resumption to pull back to 1–4, and then stood at 30–0 in the next game, the previous night's storm looked to have been sent from Adelaide. But this was not to be another great Hewitt Davis Cup comeback, and Acasuso needed just eleven minutes on the sunny but chilly Saturday morning to finish the job.

Shortly after sealing his 1–6 6–4 4–6 6–2 6–1 victory, Acasuso ran to the front row of the stand, ripped off his shirt, and threw it into the arms of Maradona, who promptly raised it like a trophy. There's no cup for winning a semifinal, but the gesture was hardly premature. Wayne Arthurs and Paul Hanley had proved a useful doubles combination in two rounds for Australia, and against an Argentinian pairing that was always going to feature the redoubtable Nalbandian, the Aussies might have won if the overall score had been 1–1. But with Argentina so clearly in the ascendant, Arthurs and Hanley were fighting the momentum as well as their opponents, and it seemed entirely natural when Nalbandian and Agustin Calleri sealed the home nation's place in the final with a 6–4 6–4 7–5 victory.

The winning smash was put away by Nalbandian, the mainstay of Argentina's team, and triggered a rush by his teammates onto the court. The home side piled on top of one another in a heap near the net, confetti in the Argentinian colors of sky blue and white floated down, and champagne corks flew across the red clay.

The win deprived the tie of the eagerly awaited grudge match between Nalbandian and Hewitt, but Nalbandian had effectively won that one. He said throughout the US Open and the build-up to the semifinal that Argentina would be 3–0 up after two days, and he was proved right. While Fitzgerald was magnanimous in accepting that his side had been outplayed, his players left Buenos Aires both mentally and physically battered. With Hewitt carrying a knee injury, Philippoussis suffering back pain, and Arthurs hampered by an Achilles tendon problem, no player could be summoned to play the second dead rubber, leaving Argentina the victors 5–0, and leaving Phil Dent the last Australian to win a Davis Cup rubber in Argentina—back in September 1977.

Yet there was no lack of interest at the Parque Roca on the final day. That interest was directed toward the live scoring system of www.daviscup.com, which kept everyone's attention as long as Tursunov and Roddick were battling away in Moscow. If the USA had won, Argentina would have been at home for the final, and the Parque Roca would have hosted its third tie of the year. Shouts of "Vamos Roddick" rang out across the media center and administrative areas, but to no avail. Roddick couldn't overcome Tursunov, and Argentina would have to travel to the snow-covered streets of Moscow in the last week of November. ●

Pictured from top:

Diego Maradona; David Nalbandian (ARG);

Left to right: Jose Acasuso (ARG), Agustin Calleri (ARG)

and David Nalbandian (ARG)

Pictured opposite:

Jose Acasuso (ARG)

DAVIS CUP CAPTAINS

The inspiration, motivation and leader of the team, the Davis Cup captain is nearly always
a former player with a wealth of his own experience in representing his country.

Name

DMITRY TURSUNOV

Born

12 DECEMBER 1982 IN
MOSCOW, RUSSIA

Turned professional

2000

Seldom does playing in the Davis Cup have such an affirming effect on a player's nationality as representing Russia has had for Dmitry Tursunov.

PLAYER OF THE ROUND

THIS IS THE MAN WHO, AT THE AGE OF TWELVE, went to California and didn't pay so much as a visit back home for ten years. In the intervening time he spent nine years applying for a Green Card, the certificate that allows non-Americans to work in the United States, but by the time he began to give up hope, he had been called up to the Russian Davis Cup team, and in both the 2006 quarterfinals and semifinals proved the country's trump card.

"Applying for a Green Card was driven by the need to set up a training base in America," he explains. "I haven't given up applying for it, but after nine years you begin to wonder whether it's ever going to happen. And to be honest I need it less now, because I'm getting a little help from the Russian federation now I'm playing Davis Cup."

Because of his long period in California, Tursunov is much more at home there than in Russia, but his visits to the country of his nationality have increased in recent years, and the Davis Cup has helped him reacquaint himself with his Russian-ness. "In Russia I'm still a bit American," he says, "and in America I'm still Russian, but that's OK—I'm happy in both cultures.

"I'm a lot more comfortable talking in English than Russian, but in the last year or two my Russian's gotten way better and I'm happy doing interviews in Russian." That's an observation backed up by those who work in Russian television. "You could tell a year ago that he was very shy speaking Russian," said Alex Metreveli, the Wimbledon runner-up from 1973 and now a commentator, in mid-2006, "but these days he chats away merrily."

After his rise up the rankings in the first half of 2005, Russia's captain Shamil Tarpischev invited Tursunov onto the Russian team for the 2005 quarterfinal against France in Moscow. "I couldn't really accept the invitation," Tursunov says, "because the tie was on clay and I'm not comfortable on clay, but we agreed that I'd play in the next tie that was staged on a faster surface."

That tie came in the 2005 semifinal in Split, in which Tursunov made his debut in the doubles. In fact his first three live rubbers were in doubles, before he was called up to make his singles debut against Richard Gasquet in the fourth rubber of the 2006 quarterfinal against France. And it proved a glorious debut, Tursunov winning 7–5 in the fifth set to seal Russia's place in the semifinals. "It was a pretty exciting feeling," he recalls with his understated dry humor. "You don't get to feel that kind of atmosphere too often. I guess I was lucky that my first three ties were away from home, because you know the crowd are going to be against you but they were all very fair crowds, and you know it's nothing personal."

After his win over Gasquet, Tursunov was still playing the "not comfortable on clay" card, saying he probably wouldn't feature in Russia's semifinal against the United States in Moscow as it would be on clay. But by the time September came around, Tursunov had posted several wins on the European clay court swing, and he got the nod for the fourth rubber, in which he beat Andy Roddick 17–15 in a glorious final set in front of several thousand adoring Russian fans.

So did that make him feel even more Russian? "I don't think's it's affected how I feel. People here are more aware of me now," he said at the Kremlin Cup in Moscow two weeks later, "but it's not as if I felt less Russian before. Deep down I'm Russian, I still feel Moscow is home, even if I have a home elsewhere. I grew up here, and I feel that that's the big factor in determining your nationality." ●

83

play-off round 22-24 SEPTEMBER

Austria defeated Mexico 5-0 PORTSCHACH, AUSTRIA—OUTDOOR CLAY

Germany defeated Thailand 4-1 DUSSELDORF, GERMANY—OUTDOOR CLAY

Czech Republic defeated Netherlands 4-1 LEIDEN, NETHERLANDS—INDOOR CARPET

Romania defeated Korea, Republic 4-1 BUCHAREST, ROMANIA—OUTDOOR CLAY

Belgium defeated Slovak Republic 3-2 BRATISLAVA, SLOVAK REPUBLIC—INDOOR HARD

Spain defeated Italy 4-1 SANTANDER, SPAIN—OUTDOOR CLAY

Sweden defeated Brazil 3-1 BELO HORIZONTE, BRAZIL—OUTDOOR CLAY

Switzerland defeated Serbia & Montenegro 4-1 GENEVA, SWITZERLAND—INDOOR HARD

PLAY-OFF ROUND

FOR THE SECOND YEAR RUNNING, THE WORLD'S TOP TWO PLAYERS found themselves in play-off round action, and they were rewarded not only with wins for their respective nations, but by their countries then being drawn to face each other in the 2007 first round. But the headlines of the play-off round were almost stolen by Thailand, who at one stage on the Friday looked like it would become only the fifth Asian nation to qualify for the World Group when it had the Germans on the ropes. ●

GERMANY v THAILAND

A FEATURE OF DUSSELDORF'S ROCHUSCLUB is that a tree grows up through one of the stands. Needless to say, the stands are built around the tree, but when the stadium is full, it gives the impression that the branches rather burst through the guests like an unwanted interloper at a party.

At five o'clock on September 22, as the late summer sun began to set over the many still-verdant trees that surround the elegant club, Thailand's players were the unwanted interlopers, as a major upset was on the cards. Tommy Haas, Germany's top-ranked player at fourteenth in the word, had lost astonishingly to Danai Udomchoke, and now Paradorn Srichaphan was two-sets-to-one up against Florian Mayer, the man deputizing for the injured Nicolas Kiefer, and someone who had never won a set in his previous two Davis Cup matches.

Just three days after the Thai military had overthrown the country's elected government and put tanks onto the streets of Bangkok, Thailand was edging closer to its first-ever place in the Davis Cup by BNP Paribas World Group. Srichaphan, who had lost all of his seven matches on clay in 2006, was playing some of the best clay court tennis of his career. But at 2–2 in the fourth set, Mayer broke, and suddenly the spell was broken. In fact, Thailand didn't win another set the entire weekend.

The pictures of the coup that had gone around the world gave a constant sense of perspective to the weekend's on-court events, and Srichaphan proved very eloquent on the subject. "I don't think it's a problem," he said as part of a clear exhortation to three of Germany's four players—Haas, Alexander Waske, and Michael Kohlmann—to stick to their plans and fly to the tour event in Bangkok the following week. "Thais are peaceful people due to our culture and history. The revolution will end without violence."

While the long-term implications of the military intervention were harder to predict, the short-term implication of Thailand's collapse at the Rochusclub was that Germany confirmed its place in the World Group for 2007. Once Mayer won the fourth set, he cruised to a 3–6 7–6(4) 3–6 6–2 6–3 victory in two hours and forty-five minutes to end a day that had seen ten sets of tennis. But while the teams were level at 1–1, Germany had the momentum.

Thailand's opportunity to cause an upset had been built on Udomchoke's 6–3 2–6 7–6(6) 3–6 6–3 win over Haas, and one of the abiding memories of the weekend will be the image of Germany's No. 1 player trudging toward the edge of the court for air. It was his fourth successive five-setter after three at the US Open, and while he took a fair

amount of criticism in the German media, the former Wimbledon finalist Wilhelm Bungert came to his defense, saying that players do sometimes need two to three weeks to recover from three long five-setters. Nonetheless, Udomchoke, ranked 113, didn't seem to have enough to damage Haas (he hadn't played on clay for three years!) yet he went for his shots and pulled off what he described as the best win of his career.

By the end, Haas could hardly move and needed an hour's treatment before discharging his media obligations. By Sunday morning, Germany's captain, Patrik Kuhnen, was still not convinced Haas was fit to play. And having picked a team of two singles players and a specialist doubles team, he had a problem.

But if this was a weekend Haas would prefer to forget, it will prove one of the highlights of Alexander Waske's career. The previous day, the doubles specialist whose infectious enthusiasm is so valuable to Germany's team spirit, had resumed his impressive partnership with Michael Kohlmann that had seen them beat the Bryan twins en route to the title in Houston earlier in the year. Waske and Kohlmann crushed the so-called "Thai Bryans," Sonchai and Sonchat Ratiwatana, 6–1 6–2 6–0 in just seventy-three minutes to give Germany a 2–1 lead.

But now the thirty-one-year-old Waske was thrown in against Srichaphan for his first live Davis Cup singles rubber. No one could claim Waske is blessed with masses of natural talent, but he makes the maximum of what he has, and by sheer belief and effort, he defied the seventy-four ranking places between his 115 and Srichaphan's 41 to see Germany into the World Group on a dramatic tiebreak that twice saw Srichaphan at set point.

"This guy is fantastic," said Kuhnen of Waske after his 6–4 7–5 7–6(12) win. "He gives everything for Germany. He always believes in himself. And I knew that he could do it."

The German team had prepared for the tie with a mountain bike tour and visit to Munich's world renowned Oktoberfest. For the 2007 first round, Kuhnen would no doubt have to find a ski trip to prepare for the visit of the 2005 champions, Croatia. ●

SWITZERLAND v SERBIA & MONTENEGRO

APART FROM BEING UNIVERSALLY RECOGNIZED AS ONE OF THE GREATEST tennis players of all time, Roger Federer is also known as a real gentleman with a strong sense of fair play. But if he feels someone is deliberately taking advantage of that fairness, Federer can bite. And after securing Switzerland's place in the 2007 World Group, he bit.

Federer had just beaten Novak Djokovic 6–3 6–2 6–3 to give Switzerland an unassailable lead against four Serbs playing for the last time under the name "Serbia & Montenegro," following a referendum in Montenegro earlier in the year in favor of secession. Djokovic had played well early on, but after going two sets down, he took an injury timeout. It failed to change the outcome of the match, but it certainly changed Federer's view of it.

"I don't trust his injuries," Federer said in his main press conference, drawing a few

Pictured opposite from top:
Michael Kohlmann (GER), left, and Alexander Waske (GER);
Novak Djokovic (SCG)
Pictured from top:
Swiss fans; Yves Allegro (SUI), left, and Roger Federer (SUI)

nervous laughs from the audience. "No it's not funny," he said admonishingly, "I'm serious. I think he's a joke when it comes to his injuries. The rules are there to be used, but not abused. But it's what he's been doing many times, so I wasn't happy to see him doing it and then running around like a rabbit again. It was a good handshake for me, I was happy to beat him."

Later addressing the Swiss German press, Federer added: "I got irritated on Friday when he put on this show in his match against Wawrinka. Ninety-five percent of players use these breaks fairly, but this isn't fair, and the rules need to be changed."

There's no doubt that, in his rise as one of 2006's breakthrough players, Djokovic had taken a number of injury breaks. His defenders drew attention to a breathing problem he has, though that only fueled suspicion that he may have been taking injury breaks to get his breath back. His detractors said he was abusing the rules, and if he were to put his ailments aside he would be a better player.

In fairness to Djokovic, his rise from 72 in the rankings at the start of the year to 21 going into the tie in Geneva's Palexpo arena had given him the burden of carrying most of his country's hopes in the tie. In fairness to Federer, he was only vocalizing what many on the tour already felt. In fairness to both men, Federer's comments didn't alter the result of a tie that was effectively decided in the doubles.

Like many teams playing a Federer-led Switzerland, Serbia & Montenegro knew that, barring a freak injury or being able to tamper with Federer's food, their only chance of victory was to win the two singles in which Federer wasn't involved, and take the doubles. The first part of the plan worked well, when Djokovic won a three-hour fifty-minute five-setter against Stanislas Wawrinka on the opening day to cancel out Federer's 6–3 6–2 6–2 win over the 92nd-ranked Janko Tipsarevic.

The second part of the plan rested on the accomplished doubles player Nenad Zimonjic teaming with the inexperienced Ilia Bozoljac to provide a suitable threat to Federer and Yves Allegro. Zimonjic is without question one of the best exponents of doubles, but the Davis Cup by BNP Paribas frequently shows up the absences in the doubles rankings, and once again Federer demonstrated that he should be counted as one of the world's top doubles players. In his best performance alongside Allegro, the Swiss were simply too strong, winning 7–6(3) 6–4 6–4.

With a Wawrinka-Tipsarevic fifth rubber potentially 50:50, the Swiss still needed Federer to beat Djokovic in the first reverse singles. Like everyone playing Federer, Djokovic went into the match hoping for a rare chance to capitalize on a substandard display by the world No. 1. But by midway through the second set it was clear Federer was on song, and whether the injury break was legitimate or not, it was never going to alter the outcome.

Because of the torn tendon in his foot that caused him to miss the Swiss Indoors event in his native Basel in 2005, Federer was playing his first competitive match on Swiss soil for a year. Several thousand fans dressed in red gave him a rapturous reception, and it took an age for the stadium announcer to introduce him, given the list of achievements that had to be read out. In addition, the Swiss team was very much a collection of Federer's mates, and his friend from kindergarten days, Marco Chiudinelli,

Pictured from top:

Janko Tipsarevic (SCG); Stanislas Wawrinka (SUI);

Nenad Zimonjic (SCG), left, and Ilia Bozoljac (SCG)

Pictured opposite:

Roger Federer (SUI)

won the dead rubber to make a winning return to Davis Cup after eighteen months out following major shoulder surgery.

The message from the Swiss was clear—they wanted Federer to know that everything would be as he wanted it, so hopefully he would play as many ties as possible. "It's a great feeling to win for your team," said Federer after his win over Djokovic. But the question still remained: was the feeling strong enough to force him to prioritize Davis Cup in his 2007 schedule? The draw for 2007 would put that to the test. ●

SPAIN v ITALY

IT WAS ALMOST LIKE AN ELECTRIC LIGHT HAD BEEN TURNED ON. From the moment he stepped out in Santander for his first home Davis Cup by BNP Paribas engagement since the 2004 final in Seville, Rafael Nadal's energy and vitality shone out over this tie, setting a pace that the spirited Italians ultimately couldn't keep up with. "I love to play Davis Cup; it's my favorite competition," he said after the first of three wins—and it showed.

Nadal was the star of a Spanish team whose lowest ranked player, Fernando Verdasco at 29th, was still nine places higher than Italy's No. 1, Filippo Volandri. A star-studded lineup doesn't always guarantee great team spirit, but under the careful guidance of Emilio Sanchez, Spain's galacticos showed they could all progress in the slipstream of Nadal's shining light.

What a card to be able to play after a shocking early setback! Tommy Robredo looked out of sorts in his 6–3 7–5 6–3 defeat to the highly impressive Volandri, whose ranking of 38 looked meaningless against the ineffective world No. 7. The joy among the Italians was mixed with the rueful recognition that Volandri seldom finds his Davis Cup form on the tour—if he did, he would be ranked much higher.

With Italy having won the Fed Cup by BNP Paribas the previous week and the soccer World Cup two months earlier, and having come so close to beating Spain in the 2005 play-off round, the Italians must have felt the gods were steering them toward a historic victory. But in stepped Nadal to crush the upstarts. Facing Andreas Seppi, the man who had beaten Juan Carlos Ferrero in five sets in the corresponding tie a year earlier, Nadal came out with all guns blazing and after less than half an hour had wrapped up the first set 6–0. Seppi got into the match in the second, but in the third it was a display of regal brilliance by the king of clay, the dual French Open champion winning 6–0 6–4 6–3.

Such was Nadal's fire in the doubles that Sanchez had to pour some calming water over his partner, Fernando Verdasco. "Rafa controls his energy very well because he's played a lot of important matches with his emotions," Sanchez explained. "I was trying to control Fernando a little more because I didn't want him to get overexcited because then you play bad. He's more expressive in a way."

So often Spain's Achilles' heel, the doubles could have proved a weakness again against Daniele Bracciali and Giorgio Galimberti, Italy's regular pair who had not lost in four Davis Cup doubles rubbers. After a high-powered Spanish start, the Italians got into

Pictured from top:

The Real Sociedad de Tenis la Magdalena in Santander;

Rafael Nadal (ESP); Filippo Volandri (ITA)

the match in the second set, but lost the third, and squandered a 5–2 lead in the fourth as Nadal and Verdasco thrusted to a 6–2 3–6 6–3 7–6(4) victory.

If there was a defining moment of the weekend, it came early in the third set of the first reverse singles. Volandri had gotten off to a great start against Nadal, taking the first set and coming close to taking a two-set lead. Nadal had then cut out his errors to level the match, but Volandri was threatening to break early in the third. Sensing the danger, Nadal upped his intensity, started spraying winners right around the court, and beating his chest on the big points. It was the warrior moving in for the kill, and Volandri suddenly found he had nothing with which to face down the threat. Nadal's 3–6 7–5 6–3 6–3 win in three hours and fifteen minutes—extending his record-setting streak of wins on clay to sixty-two—was the cue for a lap of honor to celebrate Spain's presence in the 2007 World Group.

It was the first tie to be played in Santander since the 2000 semifinals, when the Spanish team, led astutely by Alex Corretja, was on the march towards its first Davis Cup title. Over a hot July weekend, Corretja, Albert Costa, Juan Balcells, and Ferrero had beaten John McEnroe's American team 5–0. Corretja was present this time too, choosing the occasion to make the formal announcement of his retirement following a persistent eye problem that had resisted all attempts at correction. The retirement of Corretja, once the spiritual leader of Spain's Davis Cup team, came on the day that Nadal, Spain's current team leader, showed he is the country's best option in both singles and doubles.

Five days later, Spain's ball came out of the hat for the 2007 Davis Cup twinned with Switzerland. Nadal was to travel to the home of his nemesis at the top of world tennis, Roger Federer. ●

SLOVAK REPUBLIC v
BELGIUM

WHAT A DIFFERENCE A YEAR MAKES. In December 2005, the Slovak Republic hosted the Davis Cup by BNP Paribas final. In September 2006, its depleted team lost its place in the World Group at the hands of Belgium, one of only two teams from the zonal groups to be promoted for 2007.

In truth, the waning of the great Slovak era had begun before the 2005 final. Karol Kucera, who with Dominik Hrbaty had created a powerful Davis Cup nation, retired at the end of 2005. Karol Beck, who had become a mainstay of the Slovak team, was not risked in the 2005 final because he had tested positive and was likely to serve a doping suspension (which he did). That left Hrbaty as the only top-100 player from the central European nation, and against a Belgian team strengthened by the rise to 34th in the rankings of Kristof Vliegen, it was always going to take another round of heroics from Hrbaty to keep the Slovaks' place in the Davis Cup elite.

In his first match in Bratislava's Sibamac Arena since a truly heroic five-set win over Ivan Ljubicic in the 2005 final, Hrbaty once again left all on the court for his country. He beat Vliegen 2–6 6–4 6–3 3–6 6–2, but it was only part one of a three-part job.

Pictured from top:

Giorgio Galimberti (ITA), left, and Daniele Bracciali (ITA);
Fernando Verdasco (ESP), left, and Rafael Nadal (ESP)

Pictured from top:

Olivier Rochus (BEL); Dominik Hrbaty (SVK), left,

and Michal Mertinak (SVK);

Left to right: Olivier Rochus (BEL), Kristof Vliegen (BEL)

and captain Julien Hoferlin

Pictured opposite from top:

Olivier Rochus is congratulated by his girlfriend;

Dominik Hrbaty (SVK)

Belgium's top player, Olivier Rochus, ranked 31, then leveled the tie for Belgium with a 6–7(1) 6–2 6–3 6–4 win over Michal Mertinak, the Slovak who had stepped in for Beck and Kucera in the deciding fifth rubber of the final but whose ranking had plunged since then from 156 to 289. Mertinak certainly didn't disgrace himself against one of the canniest players on the tour, but his big test was to come in the doubles.

If the Rochus-Hrbaty singles was always going to be the big rubber of the tie, it was vital for the Slovak Republic to win the doubles, because Vliegen was strongly fancied to beat Mertinak in the fifth rubber. Perhaps because it was so crucial, the doubles proved to be the rubber of the weekend. Belgium's captain, Julien Hoferlin, had nominated Gilles Elseneer and the giant Dick Norman, but felt his singles players were his best bet to face Hrbaty and Mertinak. It was a fluctuating match, but the Belgians were never behind. Even in the fifth set, they broke first, only to see the Slovaks get back to 4–4. But in the eleventh game, Mertinak was broken as Rochus and Vliegen battered Hrbaty at the net, and Rochus served out a 6–2 3–6 6–3 0–6 7–5 victory.

Just as in the 2005 final, the Slovaks went into the third day 1–2 down. Knowing Mertinak was unlikely to beat Croatia's big-serving Mario Ancic had not prevented Hrbaty from delivering one of the performances of 2005, inflicting Ljubicic's sole Davis Cup defeat of the year. Here he was in the same position, knowing that a superhuman effort to beat Rochus again probably wouldn't be enough. There was no doubting Hrbaty's effort, but he came up against a player in the form of his life. The diminutive Rochus broke in the opening game, and never faced a break point in the entire match. Hrbaty denied that tiredness was a factor in his 6–2 6–3 6–3 defeat, acknowledging that he had come up against a supreme performance.

Slovak captain Miloslav Mecir, who has been at the helm since the Slovak Republic first played Davis Cup in its own right in 1994, made the point that it was no disgrace to be in Europe/Africa Zone Group I, such was the quality of the teams there. It was a fair point, but perhaps also a tacit admission that, unless Beck made an impressive comeback after his suspension, the country was facing a hard battle to return to the sixteen-nation World Group. Its third and fourth players, Pavol Cervenak and Lukas Lacko, had never been inside the top 200, Mertinak's trend was downward, and Hrbaty was twenty-eight years old.

If the delight for the Slovak Republic at qualifying for the final in September 2005 had turned to the despair of dropping out of the World Group a year later, it was the reverse for Belgium. A year earlier, Rochus and Andy Roddick were in the fifth set of an absorbing match in Leuven when a dubious line call gave the American a vital lift and helped him keep the USA in the World Group. After beating Hrbaty, Rochus said: "We have such a good spirit and a great team and we had so many tough losses, I think we deserve to be back in the World Group after all we've been through."

That team spirit would be tested against the Australians in Belgium in February 2007. ●

NETHERLANDS v
CZECH REPUBLIC

WHEN HISTORY BOOKS ABOUT DUTCH TENNIS COME TO BE WRITTEN, the 1990s era of Richard Krajicek, Jan Siemerink, Paul Haarhuis, Jacco Eltingh, and Marc Koevermans is entitled to some of the bigger chapters. But that era came to an end over the play-off round weekend of 2006, when a Dutch team looking out of its depth lost in two days to the Czech Republic.

It ended a fifteen-year stint in the World Group for the Netherlands, which saw the north-west European nation reach four quarterfinals and one semifinal. A combination of good luck and ranking-defying performances had seen the Dutch keep their place in the World Group longer than their ranking strength merited, and indeed after losing 5–0 to Russia in the 2006 first round, Raemon Sluiter suggested that the Netherlands no longer belonged in the sixteen-nation elite. With the Dutch playing against a Czech team eager to limit to one year its time outside the World Group, Sluiter's comments proved to be very accurate.

To have any chance against the Czechs on an indoor hard court in Leiden, the Dutch needed the eloquent Sluiter to beat the veteran Jiri Novak in the opening rubber. So often a big-match player, Sluiter took too long to get into the match, and by the time he did, he was two sets down. The home player gave the crowd plenty to cheer about, breaking for 5–4 in the fourth set, only to drop his serve. He then saved seven match points in a marathon tiebreak before Novak converted his eighth to run out a 6–2 7–6(5) 4–6 7–6(13) winner.

With an eye on the future, the hosts gave a Davis Cup debut to nineteen-year-old Robin Haase, but he was never likely to beat the 17th-ranked Tomas Berdych, and did well to get ten games in a 6–2 6–4 6–4 win for the Czech.

The best tennis of the weekend came in the doubles, in which Berdych partnered the newly crowned US Open doubles champion, Martin Damm, against Peter Wessels and another Dutch debutant, Rogier Wassen. It should have been easy for the Czechs, but Damm admitted that the vociferous support that Davis Cup generates narrowed the gap between the two pairs. Wessels has shown he has a great Davis Cup temperament, but has too often fallen victim to injury and was not fit enough to play singles over this weekend. He and Wassen put up a good showing together, earning compliments from the Czechs, who admitted they had not expected the match to be so tough. But the momentum as well as the quality was with the visitors, who won 7–6(4) 7–5 6–7(2) 7–6(4) to seal their place in the 2007 World Group.

In 2005 the Czechs had been the last of the original sixteen World Group nations from 1981 to lose their place. A year later, and without their highest-ranked player, Radek Stepanek, they were back among the elite, and with an emphatic win.

The best news for the hosts came just a week later, when the Netherlands' under-16 boys team won the Junior Davis Cup by BNP Paribas in Barcelona, suggesting it might not be long before the orange flags and banners are once again seen at World Group ties. ●

Pictured from top:

Jiri Novak (CZE); Raemon Sluiter (NED);

The Czech team celebrates

ROMANIA v REPUBLIC OF KOREA

THE PRESIDENT OF THE ROMANIAN TENNIS ASSOCIATION IS SICK OF BEING ASKED whether he has mellowed into respectability in late middle age. But when the president is the gifted but erratic 1970s icon Ilie Nastase, the question seems entirely legitimate. Nastase sat patiently watching his successors fight for their place in the World Group over a gray and rainy weekend in Bucharest, no doubt itching to get out onto the clay to re-create some of the drama of the 1972 Davis Cup final, in which he and Ion Tiriac so nearly beat the Americans.

The tie between Romania and Korea was never going to produce any Nastase-esque extra-curricular entertainment, but in a meeting always likely to be determined by two quality players, Romanian tennis witnessed another weekend in which the veteran Andrei Pavel demonstrated that he is a colossus when playing in the Davis Cup by BNP Paribas.

With Victor Hanescu missing due to a back injury, Pavel was always going to hold Romania's hopes in his own hands, just as Hyung-Taik Lee held South Korea's. Both won their opening singles with ease, which meant the meat of the tie would come in the doubles and the first reverse singles, both of which would pit Pavel against Lee. Rain all day Saturday ensured both matches took place on Sunday, which might have benefited the slightly younger man (Lee was thirty compared to Pavel's thirty-two). But a passion for his country burns within Pavel, and it burned a hole in the Koreans that day.

Pavel's doubles partner, the former junior doubles world champion Horia Tecau, dropped both his opening service games as Lee and Hee-Seok Chung took the first set 6–2. But a short rain delay allowed the Romanians to regroup, and when play resumed, Pavel and Tecau dominated. They had to save four set points in a fourth set that saw Lee and Chung lead 5–1, but six games on the run gave Romania victory 2–6 6–2 6–3 7–5.

Two matches in a day on clay for a thirty-two-year-old father-of-two? It was a tall order for Pavel, but in some future history of Romanian tennis, he deserves as much credit as Nastase, even if his efforts will never be rewarded with a Davis Cup final or a Grand Slam singles title.

Midway through the second set, Pavel was a set down and a break adrift, and Lee was on course to set up an unpredictable fifth rubber between two vastly inexperienced players, Victor-Valentin Crivoi and Woong-Sun Jun. With the floodlights taking over from the fading daylight and drizzle falling, the sound of the Rolling Stones' "I can't get no satisfaction" at a change of ends seemed to sum up the home mood.

Yet Pavel is a fighter, and just as people were beginning to write him off, he struck back. He broke twice to take the second set and didn't let a dropped service game at the start of the third throw him off course, steaming to a 4–6 6–4 6–3 6–2 win to keep Romania among the elite.

If Pavel had found his satisfaction just as Mick Jagger had said he couldn't get any, there was another prophetic message from the loudspeaker just before the end of the match: the Pet Shop Boys' "Go west, life is peaceful there." Not only had Pavel's determination and the support of his home crowd made life peaceful for the Romanians, but four days after seeing off the team from the east, the draw for 2007 sent Romania west to an away tie against France. ●

Pictured from top:

Hyung-Taik Lee (KOR); Korean fans;

Andrei Pavel (ROM)

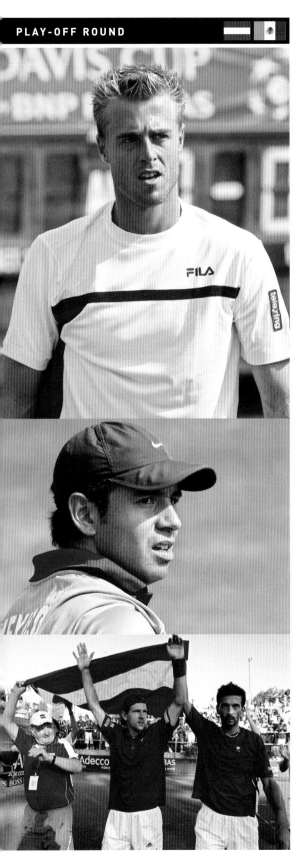

AUSTRIA v MEXICO

WHEN THOMAS MUSTER FINISHED HIS PLAYING CAREER HE DIDN'T TELL ANYONE. After a fourth-round defeat to Felix Mantilla at the French Open, he walked quietly away, saying only that he was taking a break from tournaments, and never played again. That's the way he likes it, but when you're Davis Cup captain it doesn't work that way. And ultimately, Muster's announcement that he was giving up the Austrian team captaincy to spend more time with his young family in Australia was the highlight of a weekend that was too one-sided to catch light as a contest.

It was a great achievement for Mexico to be in the play-off round, but the quality of opposition they had dismissed en route to this tie was a good class lower than the Austrian team led by a resurgent Jurgen Melzer, who had won the title in Bucharest the previous weekend. Tennis is still the second sport after football in Mexico, and the country's top players, Bruno Echagaray and Santiago Gonzalez, were junior doubles world champions in 2001. Yet the Davis Cup records of great Mexicans such as Rafael Osuna, Raul Ramirez, and others are not under threat from the best the Central American nation can produce at present.

Still, the Mexicans could have had worse draws. If they're going to play away, they'd prefer to draw a clay court nation like Austria, indeed the only thing the visitors would have liked differently would have been to play at a higher altitude. But the Austrians weren't going to take them to Kitzbuhel, and in the beautiful lower-lying lakeside setting of Portschach, the Austrians had the conditions they wanted.

For the tie to have any life in it, Mexican No. 1 Echagaray had to beat Austria's No. 2, Oliver Marach, in the opening rubber. When Echagaray took the second set to level the match and then watched as Marach had treatment to a calf muscle, the visitors were enjoying the better of the fortunes. With Echagaray 4–2 up in the tiebreak and the match over the three-hour mark, Mexico seemed to hold the cards. But once Marach had reeled off five points to take the third-set tiebreak, Echagaray's resistance evaporated, and the twenty-six-year-old Austrian ran out the winner 6–2 6–4 7–6(4) 6–3.

That merely teed Melzer up for two masterclasses, one in singles, the other in doubles. He crushed Gonzalez 6–2 6–1 6–1, and then teamed with his regular tour doubles partner, Julian Knowle, to record a 6–3 5–7 7–5 7–6(3) win in a highly entertaining match against Echagaray and Gonzalez. Knowle didn't play his best tennis, which may have contributed to the contest, but ultimately Knowle and Melzer were just too strong.

With Austria taking the two dead rubbers, Muster bowed out on a 5–0 victory, something most captains don't achieve. And to his successor, his former Davis Cup teammate Gilbert Schaller, he bequeathed a useful squad of players and a baptism of fire at home to the mighty Argentinians in February 2007. ●

Pictured from top:

Oliver Marach (AUT); Bruno Echagaray (MEX);

Austria's lap of honor

BRAZIL v SWEDEN

SIX YEARS HAD ELAPSED SINCE BRAZIL WAS A DAVIS CUP SEMIFINALIST. The world No. 1 Gustavo Kuerten had led the South American nation to a joint-best showing in 2000, before Australia on grass proved one hurdle too many. In the intervening years, Brazil had dropped out of the World Group and suffered all sorts of off-court problems. That slump coincided with Kuerten's fall from the top, two hip operations reducing the three-time Roland Garros champion to a shadow of the man who dominated on clay at the start of the decade.

But here was Kuerten back in Brazilian colors, with his country three rubbers away from regaining its place in the World Group. Kuerten hadn't played a match for seven months, he was far from match-fit, but he was back to spearhead Brazil's doubles effort. Kuerten said after the tie that the Davis Cup was important to him "to give me motivation to keep playing, practicing, and being able to live moments like those in Davis Cup." For a set the Guga magic was back, and he was clearly the best server of the quartet as he and Andre Sa took the first set on the tiebreak against the experienced Swedish pair of Jonas Bjorkman and Simon Aspelin. But the longer the match wore on, the more the thirty-year-old's lack of matches began to tell, and ultimately it was no surprise when the Swedes won 6–7(6) 6–3 6–2 7–5.

If Kuerten's limitations proved a disappointment for his nation—and ultimately contributed to a 3–1 defeat—there was at least one highlight for the hosts: Flavio Saretta's five-set victory over Andreas Vinciguerra in the four-hour opening rubber.

The court in the Expo Minas in Belo Horizonte had been laid especially for the tie, but on the Friday it took such a battering from persistent heavy rain that on Saturday morning it had to be effectively re-laid. The result was a surface that looked like clay and had the underfoot conditions of clay, but played like a hard court. And it changed the course of the weekend.

It should have played into the hands of Vinciguerra, who was in his first Davis Cup tie since the first round of 2003, when he beat Saretta in a live fifth rubber in Helsingborg. With the Swede two sets to one up this time, it looked grim for Brazil, but Saretta had the memory of that defeat to motivate him, and he came back to take the fourth set. Yet Vinciguerra led 4–1 in the fifth. Saretta came back to level at 4–4. At 5–4 Vinciguerra stood at match point as all Saretta's good work was on the point of going to waste. But the Brazilian saved the match point, broke in the following game, and served out a 6–4 1–6 3–6 6–2 7–5 victory he described as "incredible, definitely the most important victory of my life." ●

Pictured from top:

Flavio Saretta (BRA); the doubles rubber;

Andreas Vinciguerra (SWE) is congratulated by the Swedish bench

THE VITAL DOUBLES

Rarely does doubles matter more than when it's played in Davis Cup by BNP Paribas.
The result of the crucial third rubber can swing a whole tie.

Name
ROGER FEDERER

Born
8 AUGUST 1981 IN
BASEL, SWITZERLAND

Turned professional
1998

There were many admirable performances over the weekend of the eight play-off ties, but not for the first time, it was Roger Federer who was setting standards others could only dream of emulating.

PLAYER OF THE ROUND

IN HIS FIRST DAVIS CUP BY BNP PARIBAS TIE FOR TWELVE MONTHS, Federer not only played his customary three rubbers for Switzerland, but won them all in straight sets with some outstanding tennis. Federer doesn't do anything unless he does it properly, so having committed to the tie, he was there to do his very best, which in his case meant another demonstration of near-perfection.

Perhaps understandably for a man who, for the second year running, had skipped the first round because it didn't fit into his schedule, there were those who quietly questioned his commitment to the team competition. Yet Federer had said he would play at least once a year, and soon after Switzerland's defeat to Australia in the first round, the world No. 1 confirmed he would be available for the play-off tie.

He also seemed to be as happy in a team environment as he has ever been. "Because he is such a perfectionist, at times in the past Roger might have felt other team members have not taken Davis Cup as seriously as he has," says Marcel Hauck, a Swiss journalist who doubles up as press officer for Switzerland's national tennis association. "But this time he really felt everyone was doing what they could, and he felt very happy in the team. And the doubles he won with Yves Allegro was by a long way the best Davis Cup doubles the two of them have played."

A major reason for Federer feeling at one with the Swiss team was no doubt because he goes back a long way with many of the team members. He and Allegro shared an apartment together when Federer was in his late teens; he has known Switzerland's fourth team member, Marco Chiudinelli, since they were both six and living around the corner from each other in Basel; and he and the team captain, Severin Luthi, know each other from junior days. That might lead some to think Stanislas Wawrinka is something of the odd man out, but he fits into the group with great ease, and Federer was happy to listen to Wawrinka's advice on various matters over the weekend.

Although Federer's national and international profile is vastly higher than those of his teammates, he fits into the team partly because of his natural humanity that charms people the world over, and partly because it is only tennis in which he excels. In fact, Luthi made a point at the Swiss team's press conference after beating Serbia & Montenegro that he and Wawrinka had beaten Federer and Allegro at cards. Such victories over the great man are clearly to be treasured!

The only note of discord in a highly successful weekend was Federer's condemnation of Novak Djokovic's injury breaks (see page 89).

With Switzerland drawn at home against Spain in the 2007 first round, everyone connected with Swiss tennis was hoping Federer would play a full year of Davis Cup. They would clearly love him even without his usual perfectionism, but Federer without the immaculate attention to detail just doesn't exist—in Davis Cup or on the tour. ●

the final   1-3 DECEMBER

Russia defeated Argentina 3-2   MOSCOW, RUSSIA—INDOOR CARPET

THE FINAL
RUSSIA v ARGENTINA

MOSCOW, THE LOCATION FOR THE 2006 FINAL OF THE DAVIS CUP BY BNP PARIBAS, is not just the capital of Russia, but the heart of Russian-ness. When Tsar Peter the Great moved his capital from Moscow to St. Petersburg in 1712, he was trying to break from old Muscovy and establish a modern, western-looking Russian state based in the city he built as Russia's "window on the west." But Russia's heart never moved, and in 1918, a few months after the Russian Revolution, Lenin took the capital back to Moscow, knowing the move would be popular with Russia's patriotic population.

By 2006, Moscow had become a citadel of Russian tennis. Since Russia became a Davis Cup nation in its own right in 1993, only three ties had been played outside Moscow (all in St. Petersburg), and the last of those was in 1994. Every home tie since then was a Muscovite affair, and not since Pete Sampras spoiled Russian dreams by singlehandedly winning the 1995 final had Russia lost a single tie at home.

Such was the task facing Argentina in its second final. Indeed, from the moment Russia and Argentina emerged victorious from the semifinals weekend, Russia seemed an overwhelming favorite. It had home advantage against a team with a clear preference for one surface; it had a varied—if not massive—pool of committed players to choose from, and it had one of the most experienced and wily captains in the 106-year history of the Davis Cup.

And yet the closer it came to the first ball being struck, the more such strong favoritism seemed ill-founded. Yes, the Russians were at all times favored to win a second title, but the thorough preparations by the Argentinian team meant the possibility of Dwight Davis's salad bowl heading to South America for the first time could not be ruled out. For the fourth tie running, Alberto Mancini could call on the same four players: David Nalbandian, Jose Acasuso, Agustin Calleri, and Juan Ignacio Chela, and he got them to assemble in Geneva nine days before the final, where he had booked five days of practice time on a fast indoor court.

When the Argentinian players then arrived in Moscow's cavernous Olympic Stadium for their four days of practice leading up to the final, they found the court slower than the one they had gotten used to in Switzerland. Russia had opted for an older-style rubber mat surface (the court known in the 1980s as "Supreme") to give Dmitry Tursunov and Marat Safin the high bounce they enjoy, but the trade-off was that the ball came off the surface medium-fast rather than fast. For a team at its most comfortable on clay, this was a pleasant surprise and infused the Argentinian players with added confidence.

Another boost to the visitors was the noise made by their band of several hundred traveling supporters. Fifteen minutes before the start of play on the opening day, the 11,500-seat tennis arena was dominated by four blocks of pale blue and white flags and jackets, their owners screaming melodically at the top of their voices. In the middle of one block was Argentina's sporting icon, Diego Maradona, a diminutive figure with a massive presence who symbolized what a first Davis Cup title would mean to the South American nation. By contrast, Russia's fans seemed slow to get into their seats, or had perhaps been caught up in Moscow's notoriously slow-moving road traffic.

Yet for Argentina to win, it was clear Nalbandian would have to win at least two of

his three matches, if not all three. And there was a question mark over his state of mind. Just two weeks earlier, his godson Lauturo, his uncle's nine-year-old son, had been crushed to death in an elevator accident. It happened when Nalbandian was in Shanghai for the Tennis Masters Cup, and while Nalbandian played on, he was affected by the boy's death. Carrying his country's hopes in the biggest team occasion in tennis would be a severe test of character.

Even though Argentina lost, there is no question Nalbandian came through that test. He was outstanding in his opening rubber against Safin, and bounced back from a nightmare in the doubles to play a tactically astute match against Nikolay Davydenko. He then did everything possible as a supporter during the live fifth rubber to help Acasuso beat Safin, and had tears in his eyes when his teammate fell narrowly short.

But that match was part of Safin's own personal triumph. Though not as individually important to Russia as Nalbandian was to Argentina, Safin made the difference in the final.

He was taken apart by Nalbandian in the second rubber, the 6–4 6–4 6–4 score testifying to the way Safin kept himself in the match with his big serve, because frankly the difference between the players was greater. Nalbandian, often a slow starter, was focused and sharp from the outset, breaking Safin's opening eleven-and-a-half-minute service game. When the Argentinian led 5–1 in the second set it was becoming a humiliation for Safin. At that point he relaxed and briefly found some form, breaking Nalbandian and narrowing the gap to 4–5. But once Nalbandian had wrapped up the second set, the match was effectively over.

That win cancelled out Davydenko's earlier 6–1 6–2 5–7 6–4 victory over Chela. Chela had been called into action because of an impressive 5–0 winning record over Davydenko, the latest two of which had been on hard courts during Davydenko's rise to the world's top five. But Davydenko had been in the form of his life in the latter months of the year, ending up at a career-high ranking of three. In retrospect, the Russian's peak had passed by the time the Davis Cup final came around—his titles in the Kremlin Cup (played in the same Olimpiinsky arena as the final) and the BNP Paribas Masters saw him play some irresistible tennis—and his match with Chela was the least interesting of the five rubbers. Ultimately Chela was too unadventurous and Davydenko too quick and powerful for there to be any other result than a Russian victory.

Chela did stake one minor claim to a footnote in the history books. He made the first request in Davis Cup history for a point to be reviewed by electronic technology. For the first time, the Davis Cup used the Hawk-Eye Officiating system that had been introduced into top-flight tennis at the Hopman Cup and then the Masters Series tournament in Miami earlier in the year. One difference from the individual events was that the Davis Cup final allowed for an unlimited number of "reasonable requests" in a match rather than limiting them to two per set, a rule that led to more challenges early in sets but probably no more overall than under the two-per-set system. For the record, Chela's challenge failed, as did most of the challenges over the three days of the final—no doubt an indirect compliment to the line judges.

Pictured from top:

Marat Safin (RUS); Juan Ignacio Chela (ARG)

Before play began on Saturday, Alex Metreveli was honored as the recipient of the 2006 Davis Cup Award of Excellence. Metreveli, the most successful player in the history of the Soviet and Russian tennis team, was already there commentating for Russian television, and he had his achievements acknowledged in an on-court ceremony. From Georgia, Metreveli played 105 rubbers for the Soviet Union (USSR) between 1963 and 1976, winning 80 of them. Because Russia took the USSR's place in the Davis Cup World Group, Metreveli is listed as having played for Russia, because representing Georgia was not an option until 1993.

With Argentina slightly favored to win the doubles, the visitors were happier than the hosts with the 1–1 first-day score. But with Russia's captain Shamil Tarpischev having said that Safin would play in the doubles if he didn't have "too stressful a match" on Friday, any advantage Argentina had was wafer-thin. Any stress Safin had from his singles came not from the match time (two hours twenty-five minutes) but from his irritation with the court, which he said didn't help him. "The surface suits him [Nalbandian] perfectly," he said on Friday night, "but it's hard for me to move on this court and find my game." A strange admission from a home player in a Davis Cup tie.

Nonetheless Safin was nominated for the doubles, not to partner Mikhail Youzhny, with whom he had an unbeaten three-match record, but Tursunov. It wasn't a completely new partnership—the pair had played together at a couple of tour events—but it was hardly a safe nomination. Tarpischev had to hope they would click.

They clicked. They clicked so well they beat Calleri and Nalbandian 6–2 6–3 6–4 in a mere ninety-eight minutes. Tursunov was outstanding, playing the doubles match of his life, and Safin was a very able accomplice. Their initial strategy was to attack from the baseline by belting the ball at their net-based opponents. Nalbandian admitted later that he and Calleri had been ambushed by the tactic, and their confidence never recovered. They never had a break point, never got beyond 30 when the Russians were serving, and took four attempts to hold Nalbandian's serve, as the visitors saw the rubber they had felt confident of claiming disappear in a puff of smoke. Tursunov dropped just four points in his seven service games.

Knowing the final day's results, the doubles appears to have been the crucial rubber. Yet at the time, there was nothing fanciful about the Argentinians' belief on Saturday night that they could still win. Nalbandian was well able to pick himself up from his letdown in the doubles, but Argentina's fate was no longer solely in his hands. Mancini said on Saturday night he had a clear idea which of his three other players should contest the fifth rubber, and was confident the visitors could pick up two points, regardless of who played for Russia.

Ultimately Tarpischev opted for Davydenko over Tursunov to face Nalbandian, perhaps the only selection decision of the whole year he got slightly wrong. Davydenko started aggressively enough, but when he missed two break points in the third game and was then broken in the fourth, his confidence ebbed away in front of the sell-out crowd. He later said he felt "tired and painful," and he looked it. He pointed out that he had only played in Friday rubbers during 2006, and at the end of a long year he felt two matches in a weekend was too much. For a man who plays more tournaments than any other top-

Pictured opposite from top:

Argentina at a press conference; Nikolay Davydenko (RUS)

Pictured from top:

Alex Metreveli, second left, receives his Davis Cup Award of Excellence from, left to right, Jan Kodes, Francesco Ricci Bitti, and Neale Fraser;

Agustin Calleri (ARG), left, and David Nalbandian (ARG);

Dmitry Tursunov (RUS), left, and Marat Safin (RUS)

Pictured from top:

Igor Andreev (RUS) leads the Russian support;

David Nalbandian (ARG); Argentinian captain Alberto Mancini

Pictured opposite:

David Nalbandian (ARG)

RUSSIA v ARGENTINA CONTINUED

100 player, it was a reasonable point, but Davydenko, who had married his longtime girlfriend Irina Vasina six days before the final, often seems to feel the pressure in the Davis Cup more than the uplifting buzz that comes with the chance of national glory.

Whatever his reasons, only once in the match did Davydenko get his act together, and by then he was two sets down. Nalbandian, who for two and a half sets needed to do little more than vary his shots and wait for Davydenko to make mistakes, was broken in the ninth game of the third, and when Davydenko broke in the first game of the fourth, a dramatic comeback was taking shape. But the game in which Nalbandian held for 1–2 seemed to signal the end of his dip in form, and he broke three more times to run out a 6–2 6–2 4–6 6–4 winner.

For the twentieth time in ninety-four finals, and the fourth time in six years, the destination of the Davis Cup would be decided in the fifth rubber. Listeners to the live radio-style commentary on the official Davis Cup website, DavisCup.com, emailed in with expressions of their excitement and anxiety, of being unable to work or study because the action was so gripping, and of klaxons and car horns being sounded in Argentinian cities after Nalbandian won his match. It truly was a global spectacle.

By the time Nalbandian ended Davydenko's erratic display, it was clear that Safin and Acasuso would contest the decider. The other possibilities—Calleri and Chela for Argentina, Tursunov and Mikhail Youzhny for Russia—were on the bench for the entire Davydenko-Nalbandian match. (Youzhny had been a somewhat surprise nomination after injuring his ankle in St. Petersburg five weeks earlier, and even though he said the injury was completely healed, the doubles was the only match he was seriously considered for.)

The choices of each captain proved to be astute as both players put on a spectacle for another sell-out crowd. Acasuso was made to pay for a tentative opening service game, Safin's break proving the only one of the first set. By early in the second, Acasuso was into his stride, using his nimble footwork to blast forehands from his backhand wing, and when he broke for 4–2 the game was on.

The tension of the occasion could easily have thwarted the quality of tennis, but the match was played at a high standard, and in the third set the level at times became astronomical. Several points had the already passionate crowd on its feet in admiration and appreciation, and one in particular is worth putting in any video collection of great moments in tennis. It involved Safin playing a defensive lob, which Acasuso chased back, playing the through-the-legs shot with his back to the net and, remarkably, throwing up a lob with it. Safin just reached it at full stretch, only for Acasuso to recover and win the point four shots later. It was the rally of the weekend.

But though Acasuso won that little battle, he dropped serve for the second time in the set, having just recovered his first break, and Safin took a two-sets-to-one lead. With Acasuso having to have his foot taped and finding it painful to land after his serve, things were looking bleak for Argentina.

Yet Acasuso regrouped in the fourth set, relaxing a little and playing six excellent service games. Safin matched him, but was beginning to look erratic. The fourth set went into the tiebreak. The feeling was that one moment of brilliance could decide the Davis Cup.

Pictured from top:

David Nalbandian (ARG) cheers from the bench; Russian fans;

Left to right: Jose Acasuso (ARG), David Nalbandian (ARG),

and Juan Ignacio Chela (ARG)

Pictured opposite from top:

Jose Acasuso (ARG); Marat Safin (RUS) is

congratulated by his teammates

That moment seemed to have arrived on the fourth point when Safin sent a crunching backhand down the line to leave Acasuso stretching in vain. It proved the only minibreak on Safin's way to a 6–4 lead. It was match point for Russia, and on the Safin serve. He missed his first delivery. The second started a rally that saw both players slicing tentatively. Then Acasuso went for a bold forehand crosscourt, and his attempted winner landed right on Safin's sideline. The tiebreak was back on serve.

At 5–6, Safin's second match point, Acasuso missed his first serve but put in a decent second. Again both men were tentative, but Acasuso went for more of an angle. He drove Safin wide to his forehand wing, opening up the next shot, a forehand down the line that should have leveled the tiebreak at 6–6. But the Argentinian snatched at it, the ball landed in the net, and Russia had won the Davis Cup by BNP Paribas.

Both players and Argentina's captain later admitted they felt Acasuso would have been the stronger man in a fifth set. "I was having trouble with my knees and my toes," the twenty-six-year-year-old Safin said, "I'm pretty tall and pretty old, but it came out well." Whether Acasuso could have pulled off a dramatic victory will never be known, but his valiant effort helped end the tennis year on a high that seemed very necessary at the start of the week.

For the final was played amid a slightly murky political climate, both in tennis and in Russia's standing in the world. During the week of the tie, an airplane was grounded at one of Moscow's airports under suspicion of radioactive contamination following the controversial death of a former Russian agent in London the week before. And on the tennis front, the International Tennis Federation's president Francesco Ricci Bitti felt the need to combat what he perceived as some people talking up a crisis in tennis. In a news conference in Moscow, he called on officials in the game not to try to "fix something that isn't broken," and while not denying there were issues to be tackled, Ricci Bitti was keen to say that professional tennis was generally in very good shape. The excitement and good spirit of the final, together with the colorful tableau of flags and clothing that graced the Olympic Stadium on all three days, showed both tennis and Russia in a very positive light.

In the various speeches at the trophy ceremony and the official Davis Cup dinner, several people remarked that Argentina was surely destined to win the cup before long. That would have been of little consolation to the visitors, who drowned their sorrows in some high-quality Russian vodka. But the difference between the Argentinian team that reached the semifinals in 2005 and the one that went a round better in 2006 was a genuine team unity, one that was clearly withstanding the disappointment of defeat.

One experienced Davis Cup watcher remarked at the official dinner that the losers almost looked happier than the winners, and that the last time that had happened was when Spain's players reacted positively to their defeat in the 2003 final in Melbourne. A year later, Spain lifted the cup. A better consolation for Argentina, perhaps, than the best bottle of vodka in all of Russia.

Pictured from top:

Russian celebrations; Russian captain Shamil Tarpischev

Pictured opposite:

Dmitry Tursunov (RUS), left, and Marat Safin (RUS)

PROFILE: SHAMIL TARPISCHEV

IN THE DEBATE ABOUT WHO RUSSIA'S KEY FIGURE WAS IN 2006, most tennis watchers would no doubt narrow it down to either Marat Safin or Dmitry Tursunov. But the architect of Russia's second Davis Cup by BNP Paribas title was really the ever-present figure who is very much Mr. Tennis in Russia.

Shamil Tarpischev is the second-most successful captain in the Davis Cup and the most successful in team tennis. Russia's victory over Argentina was his forty-second win in sixty-three Davis Cup ties, leaving him just seven short of Neale Fraser's record of forty-nine set in the twenty-four years Fraser captained Australia between 1969 and 1993. Add to that twenty-four victories in thirty-three Fed Cup ties, and Tarpischev stands head and shoulders above all other captains.

But Tarpischev is not just any captain. Very few Davis Cup captains double up as Fed Cup by BNP Paribas supremo as well, yet Tarpischev is also the president of the Russian Tennis Federation, a member of the International Olympic Committee, and holds various other posts too numerous to mention. Born in 1948, he first captained his national Davis Cup team (then the Soviet Union) in 1974, and he held the position until 1991, when he became sports minister under the presidency of another ardent tennis fan, Boris Yeltsin.

In 1997 Tarpischev returned to the captaincy after a six-year absence in which Russia reached two finals despite Tarpischev's shoes proving hard to fill. His immediate successor, Vadim Borisov, clashed with the country's top player, Andrei Chesnokov, which resulted in Chesnokov missing the 1994 final, and Borisov was then succeeded by Yevgeny Kafelnikov's personal coach, Anatoly Lepeshin. Following Tarpischev's return, Russia embarked on an unbeaten home run that was still intact at the start of 2007.

Yet the biggest difference between Tarpischev and many other Davis Cup captains is that Tarpischev really runs the show. While some other captains owe their positions to the goodwill of their leading players, Tarpischev calls the shots. In 2006 he made a number of surprise selections, all of which proved to be inspired. He picked Tursunov to replace the tired Nikolay Davydenko on the final day of Russia's quarterfinal against France. He chose Mikhail Youzhny over Davydenko for Russia's semifinal against the USA, and again went for Tursunov in the fourth rubber, Tursunov repaying the faith by beating Andy Roddick 17–15 in the fifth set. And his pairing of Tursunov and Safin in the doubles of the final seemed to be banking on unpredictability, but he again struck gold as the two scored a highly impressive victory over Argentina's Agustin Calleri and David Nalbandian.

As befits a man who has moved in diplomatic circles, Tarpischev knows the right thing to say without giving much away. But his immense presence is the backdrop to a Russian team comfortable with its managerial structure; indeed Safin described Tarpischev as "our tennis genius" in the run-up to the 2006 final.

Nowhere was the respect for Tarpischev clearer than after the first day of the final, when Safin was venting his spleen about the surface after he had lost in straight sets to Nalbandian. In his post-match press conference, Safin admitted to having had an argument with Tarpischev midway through the match, but was quick to add: "I don't want to offend anyone, I just want to say that this is not the kind of surface which suits my game 100 percent. If captain Tarpischev took offence, I would like to apologize because I really respect him a lot. I had nothing against him, I just expressed my opinion."

When one day Tarpischev finally steps down, he will probably have set a record for a team captain that may never be broken. His shoes—which during the final were adorned with a bright red "Russia" in capital letters—will again be very hard to fill. ●

AROUND THE TENNIS

Davis Cup by BNP Paribas ties are about more than just the on-court action. They also feature entertainment, social events and a varied supporting cast, from presidents to the world's press.

In 2006, David Nalbandian played ten live rubbers and won eight of them. That he fell short of seeing Argentina to its first Davis Cup title is largely down to the mercurial brilliance of Marat Safin.

PLAYERS OF THE YEAR

IN 2005 IVAN LJUBICIC SET A RECORD by winning eleven of his twelve live Davis Cup rubbers. No one emulated that in 2006, but David Nalbandian played ten live rubbers and won eight of them. That he fell short of seeing Argentina to its first Davis Cup title is largely down to the mercurial brilliance of Marat Safin, who won the decisive point of the year for Russia, and should surely share with Nalbandian the unofficial honor of being the Davis Cup by BNP Paribas player of the year.

Both men inspire mixed emotions. Safin's happy-go-lucky approach and huge talent charm die-hard and casual fans alike, but when things go wrong, severe irritation kicks in rapidly, and frequently the racket gets it. He doesn't smash as many as he used to, but the frustration when things go wrong for such a gifted ball-striker is never far from the surface.

Nalbandian is a man who, certainly until he won the Tennis Masters Cup in 2005, had trouble motivating himself. He was happy being on the edge of the world's top ten, and didn't see much point in making the effort to go further when there were counter-attractions to practice sessions, such as fishing, fast cars, and beautiful women. To many, that signaled a healthy sense of perspective about tennis, but Nalbandian's instinctive defensiveness meant he seldom endeared himself to the media and tournament officials.

Maybe by the end of 2006 that was beginning to change—for good reasons and bad. He has always been keen to play for his country, but in 2006 he found the Davis Cup gave him an added sense of purpose that kept the motivation going. He was Argentina's Mr. Davis Cup, and kept up a remarkable record that saw him lose just three live singles rubbers in the four years and two months following his debut in the 2002 semifinals.

In the run-up to the 2006 final, Nalbandian suffered the horror of his nine-year-old cousin and godson dying in a freak accident. Exactly how that affected him is something he may well not talk about for many years, but in his dealings with the media and officials in Moscow, he generally showed a courtesy and cooperativeness that he hasn't always been known for. Perhaps the combination of the Davis Cup responsibility and his tragic bereavement had given him added perspective on life?

Nalbandian has also had to carry the can for many of his teammates in terms of speaking English. With others declining to speak a language in which they are less than comfortable, Nalbandian often has to pick up the slack, which adds to his media workload. Something similar afflicted Safin during the final—by being the only member of the Russian team to speak Spanish, he was in demand in three languages, yet he discharged all his media obligations with an air of affability.

Safin missed Russia's first round tie against the Netherlands, and was self-deprecating in the remaining three ties. After beating Richard Gasquet in five sets, he thanked Russia's captain, Shamil Tarpischev, for his confidence in picking him, given how short of match practice he was. Perhaps Tarpischev just wanted to see how Safin's uncut mass of curly hair would stand up to five sets of tethering. By the semifinals the mane had been severely shortened, and Safin's matches too. He dispatched Andy Roddick in straight sets, but still complained about "thinking too much" when he dropped serve within sight of victory. And he approached the final with a thinly veiled fear of something going wrong. "I hope we don't have to pay for the luck we had in the 2002 final," he said after the draw. By beating Jose Acasuso in the decisive rubber, he saw to it that Russia didn't have to pay. ●

WORLD GROUP

First Round 10-12 February

Croatia defeated Austria 3-2, Graz, AUT, Clay (I): Mario Ancic (CRO) d. Jurgen Melzer (AUT) 67(2) 67(4) 64 64 63; Ivan Ljubicic (CRO) d. Stefan Koubek (AUT) 62 62 64; Mario Ancic/Ivan Ljubicic (CRO) d. Julian Knowle/Jurgen Melzer (AUT) 36 36 64 64 86; Alexander Peya (AUT) d. Ivan Cerovic (CRO) 46 62 64; Stefan Koubek (AUT) d. Marin Cilic (CRO) 61 75.

Argentina defeated Sweden 5-0, Buenos Aires, ARG, Clay (O): David Nalbandian (ARG) d. Robin Soderling (SWE) 36 62 64 61; Jose Acasuso (ARG) d. Thomas Johansson (SWE) 61 61 63; Agustin Calleri/David Nalbandian (ARG) d. Simon Aspelin/Jonas Bjorkman (SWE) 62 76(4) 26 64; Juan Ignacio Chela (ARG) d. Thomas Johansson (SWE) 64 61; Jose Acasuso (ARG) d. Jonas Bjorkman (SWE) 60 61.

Belarus defeated Spain 4-1, Minsk, BLR, Carpet (I): Max Mirnyi (BLR) d. Tommy Robredo (ESP) 63 67(5) 63 63; Vladimir Voltchkov (BLR) d. David Ferrer (ESP) 63 64 63; Max Mirnyi/Vladimir Voltchkov (BLR) d. Feliciano Lopez/Fernando Verdasco (ESP) 76(2) 64 75; David Ferrer (ESP) d. Serguei Tarasevitch (BLR) 62 61; Vladimir Voltchkov (BLR) d. Tommy Robredo (ESP) 76(6) 63.

Australia defeated Switzerland 3-2, Geneva, SUI, Clay (I): Peter Luczak (AUS) d. Michael Lammer (SUI) 16 63 60 63; Stanislas Wawrinka (SUI) d. Chris Guccione (AUS) 75 36 64 76(6); Wayne Arthurs/Paul Hanley (AUS) d. Yves Allegro/Stanislas Wawrinka (SUI) 76(6) 64 46 76(5); Stanislas Wawrinka (SUI) d. Peter Luczak (AUS) 64 62 67(7) 62; Chris Guccione (AUS) d. George Bastl (SUI) 75 63 76(7).

France defeated Germany 3-2, Halle, GER, Hard (I): Sebastien Grosjean (FRA) d. Nicolas Kiefer (GER) 75 76(7) 60; Richard Gasquet (FRA) d. Tommy Haas (GER) 16 64 64 67(1) 63; Arnaud Clement/Michael Llodra (FRA) d. Tommy Haas/Alexander Waske (GER) 67(6) 63 64 61; Rainer Schuettler (GER) d. Arnaud Clement (FRA) 64 63; Tommy Haas (GER) d. Michael Llodra (FRA) 63 63.

Russia defeated Netherlands 5-0, Amsterdam, NED, Hard (I): Dmitry Tursunov (RUS) d. Raemon Sluiter (NED) 67(2) 64 76(5) 76(5); Nikolay Davydenko (RUS) d. Melle Van Gemerden (NED) 76(6) 75 64; Igor Andreev/Mikhail Youzhny (RUS) d. Raemon Sluiter/John Van Lottum (NED) 62 36 64 64; Igor Andreev (RUS) d. Jesse Huta-Galung (NED) 63 46 76(7); Dmitry Tursunov (RUS) d. Melle Van Gemerden (NED) 76(4) 76(5).

USA defeated Romania 4-1, La Jolla, CA, USA, Hard (O): Andrei Pavel (ROM) d. Andy Roddick (USA) 67(2) 26 76(8) 62 64; James Blake (USA) d. Victor Hanescu (ROM) 64 76(5) 62; Bob Bryan/Mike Bryan (USA) d. Victor Hanescu/Horia Tecau (ROM) 62 ret; Andy Roddick (USA) d. Razvan Sabau (ROM) 63 63 62; James Blake (USA) d. Horia Tecau (ROM) 61 75.

Chile defeated Slovak Republic 4-1, Rancagua, CHI, Clay (O): Fernando Gonzalez (CHI) d. Michal Mertinak (SVK) 76(5) 76(3) 63; Nicolas Massu (CHI) d. Dominik Hrbaty (SVK) 67(5) 63 61 76(4); Fernando Gonzalez/Nicolas Massu (CHI) d. Lukas Lacko/Michal Mertinak (SVK) 62 75 36 64; Paul Capdeville (CHI) d. Victor Bruthans (SVK) 64 75; Lukas Lacko (SVK) d. Adrian Garcia (CHI) 64 41 ret.

Quarterfinals 7-9 April

Argentina defeated Croatia 3-2, Zagreb, CRO, Carpet (I): Ivan Ljubicic (CRO) d. Agustin Calleri (ARG) 67(7) 57 76(6) 61 62; David Nalbandian (ARG) d. Marin Cilic (CRO) 61 61 62; Jose Acasuso/David Nalbandian (ARG) d. Marin Cilic/Ivan Ljubicic (CRO) 64 62 36 64; Ivan Ljubicic (CRO) d. David Nalbandian (ARG) 63 64 64; Juan Ignacio Chela (ARG) d. Sasa Tuksar (CRO) 36 64 76(6) 76(5).

Australia defeated Belarus 5-0, Melbourne, AUS, Hard (O): Chris Guccione (AUS) d. Max Mirnyi (BLR) 76(4) 36 75 36 64; Lleyton Hewitt (AUS) d. Vladimir Voltchkov (BLR) 62 61 62; Wayne Arthurs/Paul Hanley (AUS) d. Max Mirnyi/Vladimir Voltchkov (BLR) 36 64 57 63 75; Wayne Arthurs (AUS) d. Serguei Tarasevitch (BLR) 76(6) 62; Chris Guccione (AUS) d. Alexandr Zotov (BLR) 61 63.

Russia defeated France 4-1, Pau, FRA, Carpet (I): Marat Safin (RUS) d. Richard Gasquet (FRA) 76(4) 46 63 67(1) 61; Nikolay Davydenko (RUS) d. Arnaud Clement (FRA) 36 62 64 76(4); Arnaud Clement/Michael Llodra (FRA) d. Dmitry Tursunov/Mikhail Youzhny (RUS) 63 63 67(3) 57 62; Dmitry Tursunov (RUS) d. Richard Gasquet (FRA) 61 36 67(4) 63 75; Mikhail Youzhny (RUS) d. Michael Llodra (FRA) 62 46 76(3).

USA defeated Chile 3-2, Rancho Mirage, CA, USA, Grass (O): Fernando Gonzalez (CHI) d. James Blake (USA) 67(5) 06 76(2) 64 108; Andy Roddick (USA) d. Nicolas Massu (CHI) 63 76(5) 76(5); Bob Bryan/Mike Bryan (USA) d. Paul Capdeville/Adrian Garcia (CHI) 61 62 64; Andy Roddick (USA) d. Fernando Gonzalez (CHI) 46 75 63 62; Paul Capdeville (CHI) d. James Blake (USA) 63 64.

Semifinals 22-24 September

Argentina defeated Australia 5-0, Buenos Aires, ARG, Clay (O): David Nalbandian (ARG) d. Mark Philippoussis (AUS) 64 63 63; Jose Acasuso (ARG) d. Lleyton Hewitt (AUS) 16 64 46 62 61; Agustin Calleri/David Nalbandian (ARG) d. Wayne Arthurs/Paul Hanley (AUS) 64 64 75; Agustin Calleri (ARG) d. Paul Hanley (AUS) 60 63; Juan Ignacio Chela (ARG) d. Wayne Arthurs (AUS) w/o.

Russia defeated USA 3-2, Moscow, RUS, Clay (I): Marat Safin (RUS) d. Andy Roddick (USA) 64 63 76(5); Mikhail Youzhny (RUS) d. James Blake (USA) 75 16 61 75; Bob Bryan/Mike Bryan (USA) d. Dmitry Tursunov/Mikhail Youzhny (RUS) 63 64 62; Dmitry Tursunov (RUS) d. Andy Roddick (USA) 63 64 57 36 1715; James Blake (USA) d. Marat Safin (RUS) 75 76(4).

Final 1-3 December

Russia defeated Argentina 3-2, Moscow, RUS, Carpet (I): Nikolay Davydenko (RUS) d. Juan Ignacio Chela (ARG) 61 62 57 64; David Nalbandian (ARG) d. Marat Safin (RUS) 64 64 64; Marat Safin/Dmitry Tursunov (RUS) d. Agustin Calleri/David Nalbandian (ARG) 62 63 64; David Nalbandian (ARG) d. Nikolay Davydenko (RUS) 62 62 46 64; Marat Safin (RUS) d. Jose Acasuso (ARG) 63 36 63 76(5).

World Group Play-offs 22-24 September

Austria defeated Mexico 5-0, Portschach, AUT, Clay (O): Oliver Marach (AUT) d. Bruno Echagaray (MEX) 42 46 76(4) 63; Jurgen Melzer (AUT) d. Santiago Gonzalez (MEX) 62 61 61; Julian Knowle/Jurgen Melzer (AUT) d. Bruno Echagaray/Santiago Gonzalez (MEX) 63 57 75 76(3); Rainer Eitzinger (AUT) d. Daniel Garza (MEX) 63 61; Oliver Marach (AUT) d. Carlos Palencia (MEX) 60 61.

Germany defeated Thailand 4-1, Dusseldorf, GER, Clay (O): Danai Udomchoke (THA) d. Tommy Haas (GER) 63 26 76(6) 36 63; Florian Mayer (GER) d. Paradorn Srichaphan (THA) 36 76(4) 36 62 63; Michael Kohlmann/Alexander Waske (GER) d. Sanchai Ratiwatana/Sonchat Ratiwatana (THA) 61 62 60; Alexander Waske (GER) d. Paradorn Srichaphan (THA) 64 75 76(12); Florian Mayer (GER) d. Sanchai Ratiwatana (THA) 61 63.

Czech Republic defeated Netherlands 4-1, Leiden, NED, Carpet (I): Jiri Novak (CZE) d. Raemon Sluiter (NED) 62 76(5) 46 76(13); Tomas Berdych (CZE) d. Robin Haase (NED) 62 64 64; Tomas Berdych/Martin Damm (CZE) d. Rogier Wassen/Peter Wessels (NED) 76(4) 75 67(2) 76(4); Tomas Berdych (CZE) d. Raemon Sluiter (NED) 63 76(4); Robin Haase (NED) d. Jan Hernych (CZE) 64 64.

Romania defeated Korea, Rep. 4-1, Bucharest, ROM, Clay (O): Andrei Pavel (ROM) d. Woong-Sun Jun (KOR) 60 64 63; Hyung-Taik Lee (KOR) d. Victor-Valentin Crivoi (ROM) 61 61 60; Andrei Pavel/Horia Tecau (ROM) d. Hee-Seok Chung/Hyung-Taik Lee (KOR) 26 62 63 75; Andrei Pavel (ROM) d. Hyung-Taik Lee (KOR) 46 64 63 62; Florin Mergea (ROM) d. Woong-Sun Jun (KOR) 62 26 63.

Belgium defeated Slovak Republic 3-2, Bratislava, SVK, Hard (I): Dominik Hrbaty (SVK) d. Kristof Vliegen (BEL) 26 64 63 36 62; Olivier Rochus (BEL) d. Michal Mertinak (SVK) 67(1) 62 63 64; Olivier Rochus/Kristof Vliegen (BEL) d. Dominik Hrbaty/Michal Mertinak (SVK) 62 36 63 06 75; Olivier Rochus (BEL) d. Dominik Hrbaty (SVK) 62 63 63; Lukas Lacko (SVK) d. Dick Norman (BEL) 76(5) 63.

Spain defeated Italy 4-1, Santander, ESP, Clay (O): Filippo Volandri (ITA) d. Tommy Robredo (ESP) 63 75 63; Rafael Nadal (ESP) d. Andreas Seppi (ITA) 60 64 63; Rafael Nadal/Fernando Verdasco (ESP) d. Daniele Bracciali/Giorgio Galimberti (ITA) 62 36 63 76(4); Rafael Nadal (ESP) d. Filippo Volandri (ITA) 36 75 63 63; David Ferrer (ESP) d. Andreas Seppi (ITA) 62 62.

Sweden defeated Brazil 3-1, Belo Horizonte, BRA, Clay (O): Flavio Saretta (BRA) d. Andreas Vinciguerra (SWE) 64 16 36 62 75; Robin Soderling (SWE) d. Ricardo Mello (BRA) 60 61 64; Simon Aspelin/Jonas Bjorkman (SWE) d. Gustavo Kuerten/Andre Sa (BRA) 67(6) 63 62 75; Robin Soderling (SWE) d. Flavio Saretta (BRA) 60 63 76(4).

Switzerland defeated Serbia & Montenegro 4-1, Geneva, SUI, Hard (I): Roger Federer (SUI) d. Janko Tipsarevic (SCG) 63 62 62; Novak Djokovic (SCG) d. Stanislas Wawrinka (SUI) 64 36 26 76(3) 64; Yves Allegro/Roger Federer (SUI) d. Ilija Bozoljac/Nenad Zimonjic (SCG) 76(3) 64 64; Roger Federer (SUI) d. Novak Djokovic (SCG) 63 62 63; Marco Chiudinelli (SUI) d. Janko Tipsarevic (SCG) 64 61.

GROUP I

Americas Zone
First Round 10-12 February

Brazil defeated Peru 3-2, Asia, PER, Clay (0): Flavio Saretta (BRA) d. Ivan Miranda (PER) 62 62 63; Luis Horna (PER) d. Ricardo Mello (BRA) 64 64 64; Gustavo Kuerten/Andre Sa (BRA) d. Luis Horna/Ivan Miranda (PER) 46 76(6) 64 57 63; Luis Horna (PER) d. Flavio Saretta (BRA) 67(6) 63 62 62; Ricardo Mello (BRA) d. Ivan Miranda (PER) 76(4) 36 64 62.

Mexico defeated Venezuela 4-1, Maracay, VEN, Hard (0): Santiago Gonzalez (MEX) d. Jose De Armas (VEN) 61 60 57 64; Miguel Gallardo-Valles (MEX) d. Yohny Romero (VEN) 64 46 36 63 1210; Bruno Echagaray/Santiago Gonzalez (MEX) d. Jose De Armas/Yohny Romero (VEN) 46 60 61 64; Bruno Echagaray (MEX) d. Jimy Szymanski (VEN) 63 62; Jhonathan Medina-Alvarez (VEN) d. Miguel Gallardo-Valles (MEX) 61 ret.

Second Round 7-9 April

Brazil defeated Ecuador 4-0, Cuenca, ECU, Clay (0): Flavio Saretta (BRA) d. Giovanni Lapentti (ECU) 76(6) 64 ret; Ricardo Mello (BRA) d. Nicolas Lapentti (ECU) 57 64 64 57 64; Marcos Daniel/Andre Sa (BRA) d. Carlos Avellan/Nicolas Lapentti (ECU) 76(2) 62 63; Flavio Saretta (BRA) d. Carlos Avellan (ECU) 64 64.

Mexico defeated Canada 4-1, Mexico City, MEX, Clay (0): Miguel Gallardo-Valles (MEX) d. Frank Dancevic (CAN) 76(4) 64 46 63; Santiago Gonzalez (MEX) d. Robert Steckley (CAN) 63 36 62 62; Frank Dancevic/Daniel Nestor (CAN) d. Bruno Echagaray/Santiago Gonzalez (MEX) 57 63 76(4) 76(4); Santiago Gonzalez (MEX) d. Frank Dancevic (CAN) 64 64 64; Bruno Echagaray (MEX) d. Philip Bester (CAN) 63 76(4).

Brazil and Mexico advanced to World Group Play-offs on 22-24 September 2006.

First Round Relegation Play-offs 21-23 July

Peru defeated Ecuador 4-1, Lima, PER, Clay (0): Matias Silva (PER) d. Carlos Avellan (ECU) 46 76(5) 76(8) 62; Ivan Miranda (PER) d. Julio-Cesar Campozano (ECU) 75 64 63; Ivan Miranda/Matias Silva (PER) d. Carlos Avellan/Julio-Cesar Campozano (ECU) 64 75 62; William Lock (PER) d. Jose Zunino (ECU) 64 60; Juan-Andres Gomez (ECU) d. Leonardo Ramirez (PER) 61 62.

Canada defeated Venezuela 3-2, Granby, CAN, Hard (0): Frank Dancevic (CAN) d. Daniel Vallverdu (VEN) 62 64 62; Philip Bester (CAN) d. Jhonathan Medina-Alvarez (VEN) 75 64 26 64; Frank Dancevic/Daniel Nestor (CAN) d. Juan De Armas/Daniel Vallverdu (VEN) 61 64 76(2); Jhonathan Medina-Alvarez (VEN) d. Robert Steckley (CAN) 67(4) 64 33 ret; Daniel Vallverdu (VEN) d. Philip Bester (CAN) w/o.

Second Round Relegation Play-off 22-24 September

Venezuela defeated Ecuador 5-0, Higuerote, VEN, Hard (0): Yohny Romero (VEN) d. Julio-Cesar Campozano (ECU) 63 61 67(3) 61; Jhonathan Medina-Alvarez (VEN) d. Carlos Avellan (ECU) 06 63 16 75 30 ret; Piero Luisi/Daniel Vallverdu (VEN) d. Carlos Avellan/Julio-Cesar Campozano (ECU) 62 61 64; Piero Luisi (VEN) d. Jose Zunino (ECU) 63 64; Daniel Vallverdu (VEN) d. Juan-Andres Gomez (ECU) 63 75.

Ecuador relegated to Americas Zone Group II in 2007.

Asia/Oceania Zone
First Round 10-12 February

Korea, Rep. defeated India 4-1, Changwon, KOR, Hard (0): Hee-Seok Chung (KOR) d. Rohan Bopanna (IND) 36 62 63 64; Hyung-Taik Lee (KOR) d. Prakash Amritraj (IND) 62 62 60; Mahesh Bhupathi/Leander Paes (IND) d. Woong-Sun Jun/Oh-Hee Kwon (KOR) 62 16 63 62; Hyung-Taik Lee (KOR) d. Rohan Bopanna (IND) 63 61 62; Woong-Sun Jun (KOR) d. Prakash Amritraj (IND) 63 36 75.

Chinese Taipei defeated Pakistan 3-2, Taipei, TPE, Hard (0): Aisam Qureshi (PAK) d. Ti Chen (TPE) 62 63 64; Yeu-Tzuoo Wang (TPE) d. Aqeel Khan (PAK) 62 64 64; Aqeel Khan/Aisam Qureshi (PAK) d. Yeu-Tzuoo Wang/Chu-Huan Yi (TPE) 16 76(7) 64 67(5) 97; Yeu-Tzuoo Wang (TPE) d. Aisam Qureshi (PAK) 61 63 63; Ti Chen (TPE) d. Aqeel Khan (PAK) 46 61 64 63.

Japan defeated China, P.R. 5-0, Osaka, JPN, Carpet (I): Gouichi Motomura (JPN) d. Yu Wang (CHN) 63 64 36 46 63; Go Soeda (JPN) d. Peng Sun (CHN) 63 63 76(5); Satoshi Iwabuchi/Toshihide Matsui (JPN) d. Xin-Yuan Yu/Shao-Xuan Zeng (CHN) 61 67(6) 63 16 63; Go Soeda (JPN) d. Yu Wang (CHN) 61 61; Toshihide Matsui (JPN) d. Peng Sun (CHN) 60 46 63.

Thailand defeated Uzbekistan 3-2, Tashkent, UZB, Hard (I): Paradorn Srichaphan (THA) d. Farrukh Dustov (UZB) 64 63; Danai Udomchoke (THA) d. Denis Istomin (UZB) 64 36 61 64; Sanchai Ratiwatana/Sonchat Ratiwatana (THA) d. Murad Inoyatov/Denis Istomin (UZB) 64 26 76(4) 63; Denis Istomin (UZB) d. Sonchat Ratiwatana (THA) 76(4) 26 61; Sarvar Ikramov (UZB) d. Sanchai Ratiwatana (THA) 46 61 64.

Second Round 7-9 April

Korea, Rep. defeated Chinese Taipei 4-1, Taipei, TPE, Hard (0): Hyung-Taik Lee (KOR) d. Ti Chen (TPE) 61 64 76(3); Yeu-Tzuoo Wang (TPE) d. Woong-Sun Jun (KOR) 36 75 62 62; Hee-Seok Chung/Hyung-Taik Lee (KOR) d. Yeu-Tzuoo Wang/Chu-Huan Yi (TPE) 63 61 ret; Hyung-Taik Lee (KOR) d. Yeu-Tzuoo Wang (TPE) 26 76(7) 76(2) 60; Woong-Sun Jun (KOR) d. Chu-Huan Yi (TPE) 67(4) 76(2) 75.

Thailand defeated Japan 3-2, Bangkok, THA, Hard (0): Paradorn Srichaphan (THA) d. Gouichi Motomura (JPN) 64 76(4) 61; Danai Udomchoke (THA) d. Go Soeda (JPN) 75 36 67(4) 64 63; Sanchai Ratiwatana/Sonchat Ratiwatana (THA) d. Satoshi Iwabuchi/Toshihide Matsui (JPN) 64 63 46 62; Toshihide Matsui (JPN) d. Sanchai Ratiwatana (THA) 63 64; Gouichi Motomura (JPN) d. Sonchat Ratiwatana (THA) 61 61.

Korea, Rep. and Thailand advanced to World Group Play-offs on 22-24 September 2006.

First Round Relegation Play-offs 7-9 April

India defeated Pakistan 3-2, Mumbai, IND, Grass (0): Aisam Qureshi (PAK) d. Rohan Bopanna (IND) 76(5) 64 64; Prakash Amritraj (IND) d. Aqeel Khan (PAK) 76(5) 76(1) 64; Mahesh Bhupathi/Leander Paes (IND) d. Jalil Khan/Asim Shafik (PAK) 62 63 61; Aisam Qureshi (PAK) d. Prakash Amritraj (IND) 62 64 36 63; Leander Paes (IND) d. Aqeel Khan (PAK) 64 76(4) 36 06 61.

Uzbekistan defeated China, P.R. 3-0, Tashkent, UZB, Clay (0): Denis Istomin (UZB) d. Peng Sun (CHN) 64 62 36 63; Farrukh Dustov (UZB) d. Yu Wang (CHN) 64 60 61; Farrukh Dustov/Denis Istomin (UZB) d. Xin-Yuan Yu/Shao-Xuan Zeng (CHN) 76(5) 75 76(4); final two rubbers not played.

Second Round Relegation Play-off 22-24 September

China, P.R. defeated Pakistan 5-0, Beijing, CHN, Hard (I): Yu Wang (CHN) d. Aqeel Khan (PAK) 61 57 63 64; Peng Sun (CHN) d. Aisam Qureshi (PAK) 36 76(5) 36 63 86; Xin-Yuan Yu/Shao-Xuan Zeng (CHN) d. Aqeel Khan/Aisam Qureshi (PAK) 75 64 64; Yu Wang (CHN) d. Asim Shafik (PAK) 60 60; Peng Sun (CHN) d. Aqeel Khan (PAK) 62 60.

Pakistan relegated to Asia/Oceania Zone Group II in 2007.

Europe/Africa Zone
First Round 10-12 February

Luxembourg defeated Portugal 4-1, Esch/Alzette, LUX, Hard (I): Rui Machado (POR) d. Laurent Bram (LUX) 75 64 62; Gilles Muller (LUX) d. Frederico Gil (POR) 62 61 64; Gilles Muller/Mike Scheidweiler (LUX) d. Frederico Gil/Leonardo Tavares (POR) 46 63 75 61; Gilles Muller (LUX) d. Rui Machado (POR) 76(3) 76(2) 61; Gilles Kremer (LUX) d. Goncalo Nicau (POR) 67(8) 64 64.

Serbia & Montenegro defeated Israel 4-1, Ramat Hasharon, ISR, Hard (0): Janko Tipsarevic (SCG) d. Dudi Sela (ISR) 76(3) 26 60 64; Novak Djokovic (SCG) d. Noam Okun (ISR) 76(2) 76(6) 62; Jonathan Erlich/Andy Ram (ISR) d. Ilija Bozoljac/Janko Tipsarevic (SCG) 63 62 64; Novak Djokovic (SCG) d. Dudi Sela (ISR) 61 62 76(3); Janko Tipsarevic (SCG) d. Noam Okun (ISR) 76(10) 64.

Second Round 7-9 April

Czech Republic defeated Morocco 5-0, Oudja, MAR, Clay (0): Tomas Zib (CZE) d. Mounir El Aarej (MAR) 26 61 75 64; Tomas Berdych (CZE) d. Mehdi Tahiri (MAR) 63 61 62; Tomas Berdych/Lukas Dlouhy (CZE) d. Talal Ouahabi/Mehdi Ziadi (MAR) 63 62 63; Lukas Dlouhy (CZE) d. Mehdi Ziadi (MAR) 62 61; Tomas Zib (CZE) d. Mehdi Tahiri (MAR) 64 75.

Italy defeated Luxembourg 5-0, Torre Del Greco, ITA, Clay (0): Filippo Volandri (ITA) d. Gilles Kremer (LUX) 62 61 62; Andreas Seppi (ITA) d. Laurent Bram (LUX) 62 61 63; Daniele Bracciali/Giorgio Galimberti (ITA) d. Laurent Bram/Gilles Kremer (LUX) 63 62 64; Filippo Volandri (ITA) d. Laurent Bram (LUX) 63 61; Giorgio Galimberti (ITA) d. Gilles Kremer (LUX) 61 63.

Serbia & Montenegro defeated Great Britain 3-2, Glasgow, GBR, Carpet (I): Greg Rusedski (GBR) d. Janko Tipsarevic (SCG) 63 67(2) 75 75; Novak Djokovic (SCG) d. Arvind Parmar (GBR) 63 62 75; Ilija Bozoljac/Nenad Zimonjic (SCG) d. Andy Murray/Greg Rusedski (GBR) 63 36 63 64; Novak Djokovic (SCG) d. Greg Rusedski (GBR) 63 46 63 76(6); Arvind Parmar (GBR) d. Ilija Bozoljac (SCG) 75 64.

Belgium defeated Ukraine 4-1, Kiev, UKR, Carpet (I): Olivier Rochus (BEL) d. Orest Tereshchuk (UKR) 63 61 62; Kristof Vliegen (BEL) d. Sergiy Stakhovsky (UKR) 63 63 76(5); Olivier Rochus/Kristof Vliegen (BEL) d. Sergei Bubka/Sergiy Stakhovsky (UKR) 76(3) 63 62; Gilles Elseneer (BEL) d. Sergiy Stakhovsky (UKR) 63 76(2); Sergei Bubka (UKR) d. Stefan Wauters (BEL) 76(5) 36 76(8).

Belgium, Czech Republic, Italy and Serbia & Montenegro advanced to World Group Play-offs on 22-24 September 2006.

121

First Round Relegation Play-off 21-23 July

Israel defeated Great Britain 3-2, Eastbourne, GBR, Grass (0): Noam Okun (ISR) d. Alex Bogdanovic (GBR) 64 75 62; Andy Murray (GBR) d. Andy Ram (ISR) 26 46 75 62 63; Jonathan Erlich/Andy Ram (ISR) d. Jamie Delgado/Andy Murray (GBR) 36 63 57 63 64; Noam Okun (ISR) d. Jamie Delgado (GBR) 63 64 67(5) 26 63; Alan Mackin (GBR) d. Dekel Valtzer (ISR) 62 61.

Second Round Relegation Play-offs 22-24 September

Portugal defeated Morocco 3-2; Marrakech, MAR, Clay (0): Rabie Chaki (MAR) d. Goncalo Nicau (POR) 46 63 16 63 1210; Frederico Gil (POR) d. Mehdi Tahiri (MAR) 62 64 62; Frederico Gil/Goncalo Nicau (POR) d. Mounir El Aarej/Mehdi Ziadi (MAR) 61 63 61; Frederico Gil (POR) d. Rabie Chaki (MAR) 16 75 61 76(5); Mehdi Tahiri (MAR) d. Pedro Sousa (POR) 76(2) 46 62.

Great Britain defeated Ukraine 3-2, Odessa, UKR, Clay (0): Greg Rusedski (GBR) d. Sergiy Stakhovsky (UKR) 16 63 57 64 97; Andy Murray (GBR) d. Aleksandr Dolgopolov (UKR) 63 64 62; Sergiy Stakhovsky/Orest Tereshchuk (UKR) d. Jamie Delgado/Andy Murray (GBR) 63 63 63; Andy Murray (GBR) d. Sergiy Stakhovsky (UKR) 63 62 75; Sergei Bubka (UKR) d. Jamie Baker (GBR) 63 76(6).

Morocco and Ukraine relegated to Europe/Africa Zone Group II in 2007.

GROUP II

Americas Zone
First Round 10-12 February

Paraguay defeated Bolivia 4-1, Santa Cruz de la Sierra, BOL, Clay (0): Emilio Baez-Britez (PAR) d. Mauricio Estivariz (BOL) 63 63 61; Ramon Delgado (PAR) d. Jose-Roberto Velasco (BOL) 60 62 64; Emilio Baez-Britez/Ramon Delgado (PAR) d. Jose Antelo/Mauricio Estivariz (BOL) 62 75 62; Lorenzo Gonzalez (PAR) d. Carlos Alvarez (BOL) 16 76(6) 62; Jose-Roberto Velasco (BOL) d. Juan-Carlos Ramirez (PAR) 62 46 61.

Colombia defeated Uruguay 4-1, Bogota, COL, Clay (0): Alejandro Falla (COL) d. Marcel Felder (URU) 62 61 62; Santiago Giraldo (COL) d. Pablo Cuevas (URU) 64 76(4) 76(3); Alejandro Falla/Carlos Salamanca (COL) d. Pablo Cuevas/Martin Vilarrubi (URU) 46 57 62 64 63; Martin Vilarrubi (URU) d. Pablo Gonzalez (COL) 76(6) 61; Carlos Salamanca (COL) d. Federico Sansonetti (URU) 63 61.

Netherlands Antilles defeated Guatemala 3-2, Emmastad, AHO, Hard (0): Jean-Julien Rojer (AHO) d. Israel Morales (GUA) 63 62 61; Cristian Paiz (GUA) d. Rasid Winklaar (AHO) 36 64 76(5) 57 64; Raoul Behr/Jean-Julien Rojer (AHO) d. Cristian Paiz/Luis Perez-Chete (GUA) 64 76(3) 63; Jean-Julien Rojer (AHO) d. Cristian Paiz (GUA) 61 62 63; Israel Morales (GUA) d. Alexander Blom (AHO) 16 61 66 ret.

Dominican Republic defeated Jamaica 5-0, Santiago, DOM, Clay (0): Jhonson Garcia (DOM) d. Scott Willinsky (JAM) 61 63 60; Victor Estrella (DOM) d. Ryan Russell (JAM) 63 62 60; Victor Estrella/Jhonson Garcia (DOM) d. Ryan Russell/Jermaine Smith (JAM) 63 63 75; Henry Estrella (DOM) d. Elvis Henry (JAM) 36 64 62; Jesus Francisco Felix (DOM) d. Scott Willinsky (JAM) 62 67(3) 63.

Second Round 7-9 April

Colombia defeated Paraguay 4-1: Bogota, COL, Clay (0): Ramon Delgado (PAR) d. Santiago Giraldo (COL) 26 46 76(1) 76(4) 108; Alejandro Falla (COL) d. Emilio Baez-Britez (PAR) 62 57 60 63; Alejandro Falla/Carlos Salamanca (COL) d. Ramon Delgado/Francisco Rodriguez (PAR) 75 36 66 def; Alejandro Falla (COL) d. Francisco Rodriguez (PAR) 60 61 63; Pablo Gonzalez (COL) d. Emilio Baez-Britez (PAR) 62 61.

Dominican Republic defeated Netherlands Antilles 3-2, Emmastad, AHO, Hard (0): Jean-Julien Rojer (AHO) d. Victor Estrella (DOM) 61 67(1) 75 61; Jhonson Garcia (DOM) d. Alexander Blom (AHO) 60 63 61; Victor Estrella/Jhonson Garcia (DOM) d. Raoul Behr/Jean-Julien Rojer (AHO) 76(3) 64 64; Jean-Julien Rojer (AHO) d. Jhonson Garcia (DOM) 63 36 67(4) 62 64; Victor Estrella (DOM) d. Rasid Winklaar (AHO) 62 63 75.

Third Round 22-24 September

Colombia defeated Dominican Republic 5-0, Santo Domingo, DOM, Hard (0): Alejandro Falla (COL) d. Jhonson Garcia (DOM) 62 63 61; Santiago Giraldo (COL) d. Victor Estrella (DOM) 61 57 64 40 ret; Alejandro Falla/Carlos Salamanca (COL) d. Victor Estrella/Jhonson Garcia (DOM) 64 64 64; Pablo Gonzalez (COL) d. Jesus Francisco Felix (DOM) 60 61; Santiago Giraldo (COL) d. Jose Hernandez (DOM) 67(9) 63 61.

Colombia promoted to Americas Zone Group I in 2007.

Relegation Play-offs 7-9 April

Uruguay defeated Bolivia 5-0, Salto, URU, Clay (0): Pablo Cuevas (URU) d. Jose-Roberto Velasco (BOL) 62 62 26 62; Martin Vilarrubi (URU) d. Mauricio Estivariz (BOL) 36 64 62 62; Pablo Cuevas/Marcel Felder (URU) d. Carlos Alvarez/Jose-Roberto Velasco (BOL) 60 64 62; Marcel Felder (URU) d. Mauricio Estivariz (BOL) 60 62; Federico Sansonetti (URU) d. Jorge Villanueva (BOL) 61 61.

Jamaica defeated Guatemala 3-2, Montego Bay, JAM, Hard (0): Ryan Russell (JAM) d. Israel Morales (GUA) 64 63 62; Cristian Paiz (GUA) d. Damion Johnson (JAM) 64 64 57 63; Ryan Russell/Jermaine Smith (JAM) d. Manuel Chavez/Luis Perez-Chete (GUA) 76(5) 63 61; Ryan Russell (JAM) d. Cristian Paiz (GUA) 63 60 30 ret; Israel Morales (GUA) d. Eldad Campbell (JAM) 64 61.

Bolivia and Guatemala relegated to Americas Zone Group III in 2007.

Asia/Oceania Zone
First Round 10-12 February

New Zealand defeated Lebanon 5-0, Auckland, NZL, Hard (I): Mark Nielsen (NZL) d. Karim Alayli (LIB) 62 61 62; Daniel King-Turner (NZL) d. Patrick Chucri (LIB) 63 62 61; Daniel King-Turner/Mark Nielsen (NZL) d. Karim Alayli/Patrick Chucri (LIB) 62 63 61; Jose Statham (NZL) d. Wahib Maknieh (LIB) 64 63; Daniel King-Turner (NZL) d. Karim Alayli (LIB) 63 64.

Kazakhstan defeated Kuwait 3-2, Kuwait City, KUW, Hard (0): Mohammed Al Ghareeb (KUW) d. Dmitri Makeyev (KAZ) 64 64 75; Alexey Kedriouk (KAZ) d. Abdullah Magdas (KUW) 64 61 75; Alexey Kedriouk/Dmitri Makeyev (KAZ) d. Mohammed Al Ghareeb/Mohammad-Khaliq Siddiq (KUW) 46 75 64 36 62; Mohammed Al Ghareeb (KUW) d. Alexey Kedriouk (KAZ) 63 67(4) 46 62 119; Dmitri Makeyev (KAZ) d. Abdullah Magdas (KUW) 62 76(1) 36 60.

Hong Kong, China defeated Pacific Oceania 4-1, Causeway Bay, HKG, Hard (0): Wing-Luen Wong (HKG) d. Michael Leong (POC) 64 46 62 64; West Nott (POC) d. Hiu-Tung Yu (HKG) 76(10) 64 64; Martin Sayer/Wing-Luen Wong (HKG) d. Michael Leong/West Nott (POC) 16 63 64 62; Hiu-Tung Yu (HKG) d. Juan Sebastien Langton (POC) 62 63 60; Xiao-Peng Lai (HKG) d. Brett Baudinet (POC) 46 64 64.

Indonesia defeated Malaysia 5-0, East Kalimantan, INA, Hard (0): Suwandi Suwandi (INA) d. Abdul-Hazli Bin Zainuddin (MAS) 61 62 62; Prima Simpatiaji (INA) d. Razlan Rawi (MAS) 61 60 61; Faisal Aidil/Suwandi Suwandi (INA) d. Muhd-Ashaari Bin Zainal-Abidin/Abdul-Hazli Bin Zainuddin (MAS) 60 61 60; Elbert Sie (INA) d. Mohammed-Faizal Bin Othman (MAS) 61 60; Faisal Aidil (INA) d. Muhd-Ashaari Bin Zainal-Abidin (MAS) 61 64.

Second Round 7-9 April

Kazakhstan defeated New Zealand 3-2, Almaty, KAZ, Hard (I): Alexey Kedriouk (KAZ) d. Adam Thompson (NZL) 62 63 61; Dmitri Makeyev (KAZ) d. Daniel King-Turner (NZL) 64 64 36 63; Alexey Kedriouk/Dmitri Makeyev (KAZ) d. Alistair Hunt/Daniel King-Turner (NZL) 75 64 67(6) 76(5); Jose Statham (NZL) d. Igor Chaldounov (KAZ) 61 62; Adam Thompson (NZL) d. Vitaley Pavlov (KAZ) 60 63.

Indonesia defeated Hong Kong, China 5-0, Surabaya, INA, Hard (0): Prima Simpatiaji (INA) d. Wing-Luen Wong (HKG) 64 63 26 63; Febi Widhiyanto (INA) d. Hiu-Tung Yu (HKG) 63 64 64; Suwandi Suwandi/Bonit Wiryawan (INA) d. Wing-Luen Wong/Hiu-Tung Yu (HKG) 16 63 64 36 62; Prima Simpatiaji (INA) d. Xiao-Peng Lai (HKG) 75 62; Febi Widhiyanto (INA) d. Jason Sankey (HKG) 63 60.

Third Round 22-24 September

Kazakhstan defeated Indonesia 3-2, Almaty, KAZ, Hard (I): Suwandi Suwandi (INA) d. Dmitri Makeyev (KAZ) 63 64 64; Alexey Kedriouk (KAZ) d. Prima Simpatiaji (INA) 63 67(2) 64 76(3); Suwandi Suwandi/Bonit Wiryawan (INA) d. Alexey Kedriouk/Anton Tsymbalov (KAZ) 57 63 63 76(7); Alexey Kedriouk (KAZ) d. Elbert Sie (INA) 62 64 62; Anton Tsymbalov (KAZ) d. Prima Simpatiaji (INA) 76(2) 64 36 63.

Kazakhstan promoted to Asia/Oceania Zone Group I in 2007.

Relegation Play-offs 7-9 April

Kuwait defeated Lebanon 5-0, Jounieh, LIB, Clay (0): Abdullah Magdas (KUW) d. Antoine Breikeh (LIB) 61 61 61; Mohammed Al Ghareeb (KUW) d. John El Khoury (LIB) 63 61 60; Mohammed Al Ghareeb/Mohammad-Khaliq Siddiq (KUW) d. Georgio Bedran/Antoine Breikeh (LIB) 61 61 63; Ahmed Rabeea (KUW) d. Georgio Bedran (LIB) 61 64; Abdullah Magdas (KUW) d. Ibrahim Abou Chahine (LIB) 61 60.

Pacific Oceania defeated Malaysia 3-2, New Caledonia, POC, Hard (0): Yew-Ming Si (MAS) d. West Nott (POC) 26 16 12 ret; Michael Leong (POC) d. Selvam Veerasingam (MAS) 63 63 61; Yew-Ming Si/Selvam Veerasingam (MAS) d. Brett Baudinet/Juan Sebastien Langton (POC) 64 76(6) 36 76(3); Michael Leong (POC) d. Yew-Ming Si (MAS) 63 62 62; Juan Sebastien Langton (POC) d. Selvam Veerasingam (MAS) 62 61 45 ret.

Lebanon and Malaysia relegated to Asia/Oceania Zone Group III in 2007.

Europe/Africa Zone
First Round 7-9 April

Norway defeated Zimbabwe 4-1, Harare, ZIM, Hard (O): Jan-Frode Andersen (NOR) d. Genius Chidzikwe (ZIM) 64 62 57 76(3); Stian Boretti (NOR) d. Gwinyai Tongoona (ZIM) 60 63 63; Genius Chidzikwe/Gwinyai Tongoona (ZIM) d. Jan-Frode Andersen/Stian Boretti (NOR) 63 62 36 64; Stian Boretti (NOR) d. Genius Chidzikwe (ZIM) 46 75 75 36 63; Carl Sundberg (NOR) d. Stefan D'Almeida (ZIM) 63 61.

Macedonia, F.Y.R. defeated Greece 4-1, Athens, GRE, Clay (O): Konstantinos Economidis (GRE) d. Predrag Rusevski (MKD) 76(5) 57 64 67(5) 64; Lazar Magdincev (MKD) d. Alexander Jakupovic (GRE) 76(4) 60 62; Lazar Magdincev/Predrag Rusevski (MKD) d. Alexander Jakupovic/Nikos Rovas (GRE) 36 63 64 62; Lazar Magdincev (MKD) d. Nikos Rovas (GRE) 62 76(3) 61; Predrag Rusevski (MKD) d. Paris Gemouchidis (GRE) 61 76(3).

Finland defeated Ireland 3-2, Helsinki, FIN, Hard (I): Jarkko Nieminen (FIN) d. Kevin Sorensen (IRL) 64 64 62; Louk Sorensen (IRL) d. Juho Paukku (FIN) 64 62 63; Tuomas Ketola/Jarkko Nieminen (FIN) d. Tristan Farron-Mahon/Kevin Sorensen (IRL) 60 63 62; Jarkko Nieminen (FIN) d. Louk Sorensen (IRL) 64 61 60; Kevin Sorensen (IRL) d. Juho Paukku (FIN) 64 62.

Algeria defeated Slovenia 3-2, Algiers, ALG, Clay (O): Slimane Saoudi (ALG) d. Rok Jarc (SLO) 64 64 36 61; Lamine Ouahab (ALG) d. Grega Zemlja (SLO) 63 26 46 63 64; Lamine Ouahab/Slimane Saoudi (ALG) d. Rok Jarc/Grega Zemlja (SLO) 62 62 64; Grega Zemlja (SLO) d. Slimane Saoudi (ALG) 75 62; Blaz Kavcic (SLO) d. Rachid Baba-Aissa (ALG) 60 61.

Hungary defeated Egypt 5-0, Hodmezovasarhely, HUN, Hard (O): Sebo Kiss (HUN) d. Karim Maamoun (EGY) 63 64 61; Kornel Bardoczky (HUN) d. Sherif Sabry (EGY) 76(4) 61 63; Kornel Bardoczky/Gergely Kisgyorgy (HUN) d. Karim Maamoun/Mohammed Maamoun (EGY) 64 76(5) 64; Kornel Bardoczky (HUN) d. Mohammed Maamoun (EGY) 75 63; Sebo Kiss (HUN) d. Sherif Sabry (EGY) 64 63.

Bulgaria defeated Cyprus 3-2, Plovdiv, BUL, Clay (O): Marcos Baghdatis (CYP) d. Yordan Kanev (BUL) 61 62 62; Ilia Kushev (BUL) d. Fotos Kallias (CYP) 63 62 75; Ilia Kushev/Ivaylo Traykov (BUL) d. Marcos Baghdatis/Fotos Kallias (CYP) 46 63 26 76(1) 60; Marcos Baghdatis (CYP) d. Ilia Kushev (BUL) 63 62 62; Todor Enev (BUL) d. Fotos Kallias (CYP) 76(2) 61 16 64.

Poland defeated Latvia 5-0, Puszczykowo, POL, Carpet (I): Michal Przysiezny (POL) d. Ernests Gulbis (LAT) 36 76(6) 76(4) 76(7); Lukasz Kubot (POL) d. Andis Juska (LAT) 64 76(3) 67(6) 36 86; Mariusz Fyrstenberg/Marcin Matkowski (POL) d. Ernests Gulbis/Andis Juska (LAT) 63 76(4) 61; Mariusz Fyrstenberg (POL) d. Deniss Pavlovs (LAT) 63 62; Michal Przysiezny (POL) d. Karlis Lejnieks (LAT) 62 76(1).

Georgia defeated South Africa 3-2, Tbilisi, GEO, Carpet (I): Irakli Labadze (GEO) d. Izak Van Der Merwe (RSA) 64 57 36 61 63; Wesley Moodie (RSA) d. Lado Chikhladze (GEO) 76(7) 67(2) 46 76(5) 63; Lado Chikhladze/Irakli Labadze (GEO) d. Jeff Coetzee/Wesley Moodie (RSA) 64 64 76(4); Wesley Moodie (RSA) d. Irakli Labadze (GEO) 75 46 46 63 1311; Lado Chikhladze (GEO) d. Izak Van Der Merwe (RSA) 62 64 63.

Second Round 21-23 July

Macedonia, F.Y.R. defeated Norway 3-2, Oslo, NOR, Clay (O): Predrag Rusevski (MKD) d. Stian Boretti (NOR) 62 60 10 ret; Jan-Frode Andersen (NOR) d. Lazar Magdincev (MKD) 46 63 75 36 62; Lazar Magdincev/Predrag Rusevski (MKD) d. Jan-Frode Andersen/Erling Tveit (NOR) 64 76(5) 63; Lazar Magdincev (MKD) d. Erling Tveit (NOR) 64 57 62 67(4) 62; Carl Sundberg (NOR) d. Dimitar Grabulovski (MKD) 76(4) 64.

Finland defeated Algeria 4-1, Hanko, FIN, Clay (O): Timo Nieminen (FIN) d. Slimane Saoudi (ALG) 76(6) 76(5) 63; Jarkko Nieminen (FIN) d. Abdel-Hak Hameurlaine (ALG) 60 60 61; Tuomas Ketola/Jarkko Nieminen (FIN) d. Abdel-Hak Hameurlaine/Slimane Saoudi (ALG) 61 36 62 64; Jarkko Nieminen (FIN) d. Slimane Saoudi (ALG) 62 61; Abdel-Hak Hameurlaine (ALG) d. Lauri Kiiski (FIN) 64 62.

Hungary defeated Bulgaria 3-2, Plovdiv, BUL, Clay (O): Kornel Bardoczky (HUN) d. Ilia Kushev (BUL) 75 63 60; Sebo Kiss (HUN) d. Ivaylo Traykov (BUL) 63 63 63; Kornel Bardoczky/Gergely Kisgyorgy (HUN) d. Yordan Kanev/Ivaylo Traykov (BUL) 46 64 64 67(3) 119; Todor Enev (BUL) d. Denes Lukacs (HUN) 63 75; Ilia Kushev (BUL) d. Sebo Kiss (HUN) 75 16 62.

Georgia defeated Poland 3-2, Gdynia, POL, Clay (O): Irakli Labadze (GEO) d. Michal Przysiezny (POL) 36 63 64 64; Lukasz Kubot (POL) d. Lado Chikhladze (GEO) 75 64 62; Mariusz Fyrstenberg/Marcin Matkowski (POL) d. Lado Chikhladze/Irakli Labadze (GEO) 61 62 64; Irakli Labadze (GEO) d. Lukasz Kubot (POL) 46 63 57 62 64; Lado Chikhladze (GEO) d. Mariusz Fyrstenberg (POL) 75 76(3) 76(6).

Third Round 22-24 September

Macedonia, F.Y.R. defeated Finland 3-2; Skopje, MKD, Clay (O): Jarkko Nieminen (FIN) d. Predrag Rusevski (MKD) 46 61 63 36 64; Lazar Magdincev (MKD) d. Timo Nieminen (FIN) 64 62 26 76(1); Lazar Magdincev/Predrag Rusevski (MKD) d. Tuomas Ketola/Jarkko Nieminen (FIN) 63 62 36 16 62; Jarkko Nieminen (FIN) d. Lazar Magdincev (MKD) 63 60 61; Predrag Rusevski (MKD) d. Timo Nieminen (FIN) 64 64 26 46 64.

Georgia defeated Hungary 3-2, Budapest, HUN, Clay (O): Sebo Kiss (HUN) d. Irakli Labadze (GEO) 61 63 26 64; Kornel Bardoczky (HUN) d. Lado Chikhladze (GEO) 64 67(4) 61 62; Lado Chikhladze/Irakli Labadze (GEO) d. Kornel Bardoczky/Gergely Kisgyorgy (HUN) 46 60 63 62; Irakli Labadze (GEO) d. Kornel Bardoczky (HUN) 76(4) 61 67(2) 16 64; Lado Chikhladze (GEO) d. Sebo Kiss (HUN) 76(3) 76(4) 67(4) 62.

Georgia and Macedonia, F.Y.R. promoted to Europe/Africa Zone Group I in 2007.

Relegation Play-offs 21-23 July

Greece defeated Zimbabwe 4-1, Thessaloniki, GRE, Clay (O): Konstantinos Economidis (GRE) d. Pfungwa Mahefu (ZIM) 62 60 60; Alexander Jakupovic (GRE) d. Genius Chidzikwe (ZIM) 67(3) 61 75 62; Konstantinos Economidis/Alexander Jakupovic (GRE) d. Genius Chidzikwe/Gwinyai Tongoona (ZIM) 62 61 62; Genius Chidzikwe (ZIM) d. Paris Gemouchidis (GRE) 62 64; Alexander Jakupovic (GRE) d. Gwinyai Tongoona (ZIM) 62 62.

Slovenia defeated Ireland 4-1, Dublin, IRL, Grass (O): Grega Zemlja (SLO) d. Kevin Sorensen (IRL) 62 75 61; Marko Tkalec (SLO) d. Conor Niland (IRL) 46 62 46 64 63; Luka Gregorc/Grega Zemlja (SLO) d. James Clusky/Kevin Sorensen (IRL) 67(7) 63 36 63 75; Grega Zemlja (SLO) d. Conor Niland (IRL) 64 62; Stephen Nugent (IRL) d. Martin Rmus (SLO) 16 76(9) 61.

Cyprus defeated Egypt 3-2, Cairo, EGY, Clay (O): Karim Maamoun (EGY) d. Christopher Koutrouzas (CYP) 61 62 60; Marcos Baghdatis (CYP) d. Mohammed Maamoun (EGY) 64 63 64; Marcos Baghdatis/Fotos Kallias (CYP) d. Karim Maamoun/Mohammed Maamoun (EGY) 63 63 64; Marcos Baghdatis (CYP) d. Karim Maamoun (EGY) 63 64 63; Sherif Sabry (EGY) d. Petros Baghdatis (CYP) 63 62.

Latvia defeated South Africa 3-2, Jurmala, LAT, Clay (O): Andis Juska (LAT) d. Rik De Voest (RSA) 67(3) 61 64 62; Ernests Gulbis (LAT) d. Fritz Wolmarans (RSA) 75 62 64; Ernests Gulbis/Andis Juska (LAT) d. Chris Haggard/Izak Van Der Merwe (RSA) 62 46 63 62; Izak Van Der Merwe (RSA) d. Deniss Pavlovs (LAT) 63 64; Fritz Wolmarans (RSA) d. Karlis Lejnieks (LAT) 60 60.

Egypt, Ireland, South Africa and Zimbabwe relegated to Europe/Africa Zone Group III in 2007.

GROUP III

Americas Zone

Date: 14-18 June **Venue:** San Salvador, El Salvador **Surface:** Clay (O)
Group A: Bahamas, Honduras, Puerto Rico, Trinidad & Tobago
Group B: Costa Rica, Cuba, El Salvador, Haiti

Group A
14 June Trinidad & Tobago defeated Honduras 3-0: Shane Stone (TRI) d. Jose Moncada (HON) 67(4) 76(2) 63; Richard Brown (TRI) d. Calton Alvarez (HON) 63 62; Shane Stone/Troy Stone (TRI) d. Carlos Caceres/Franklin Garcia (HON) 63 60.

Bahamas defeated Puerto Rico 3-0: Marvin Rolle (BAH) d. Ricardo Gonzalez-Diaz (PUR) 63 57 63; Devin Mullings (BAH) d. Gilberto Alvarez (PUR) 63 67(3) 64; Devin Mullings/Marvin Rolle (BAH) d. Gabriel Montilla/Jorge Rangel (PUR) 64 64.

15 June Bahamas defeated Trinidad & Tobago 2-1: Marvin Rolle (BAH) d. Shane Stone (TRI) 63 36 63; Devin Mullings (BAH) d. Richard Brown (TRI) 61 64; Shane Stone/Troy Stone (TRI) d. Devin Mullings/Marvin Rolle (BAH) 36 63 64.

Puerto Rico defeated Honduras 3-0: Gilberto Alvarez (PUR) d. Jose Moncada (HON) 61 46 62; Jorge Rangel (PUR) d. Calton Alvarez (HON) 60 62; Ricardo Gonzalez-Diaz/Gabriel Montilla (PUR) d. Franklin Garcia/Jose Moncada (HON) 75 62.

16 June Puerto Rico defeated Trinidad & Tobago 3-0: Ricardo Gonzalez-Diaz (PUR) d. Shane Stone (TRI) 61 62; Jorge Rangel (PUR) d. Richard Brown (TRI) 62 67(2) 64; Ricardo Gonzalez-Diaz/Gabriel Montilla (PUR) d. Michael Clarke/Troy Stone (TRI) 63 62.

Honduras defeated Bahamas 2-1: Jose Moncada (HON) d. Christopher Eldon (BAH) 64 26 62; Calton Alvarez (HON) d. H'Cone Thompson (BAH) 64 16 75; Christopher Eldon/H'Cone Thompson (BAH) d. Carlos Caceres/Jose Moncada (HON) 64 67(7) 62.

Group B

14 June El Salvador defeated Cuba 2-1: Edgar Hernandez-Perez (CUB) d. Jaime Cuellar (ESA) 75 61; Rafael Arevalo-Gonzalez (ESA) d. Ricardo Chile-Fonte (CUB) 64 46 61; Rafael Arevalo-Gonzalez/Jaime Cuellar (ESA) d. Ricardo Chile-Fonte/Sandor Martinez-Breijo (CUB) 67(3) 64 64.

Haiti defeated Costa Rica 2-1: Gael Gaetjens (HAI) d. Fernando Martinez-Manrique (CRC) 76(4) 36 64; Juan-Antonio Marin (CRC) d. Joel Allen (HAI) 61 60; Joel Allen/Gael Gaetjens (HAI) d. Federico Camacho/Juan-Antonio Marin (CRC) 62 75.

15 June Cuba defeated Costa Rica 2-1: Edgar Hernandez-Perez (CUB) d. Federico Camacho (CRC) 61 63; Juan-Antonio Marin (CRC) d. Ricardo Chile-Fonte (CUB) 63 61; Ricardo Chile-Fonte/Sandor Martinez-Breijo (CUB) d. Juan-Antonio Marin/Fernando Martinez-Manrique (CRC) 64 61.

El Salvador defeated Haiti 3-0: Jaime Cuellar (ESA) d. Jean Marc Bazanne (HAI) 61 64; Rafael Arevalo-Gonzalez (ESA) d. Gael Gaetjens (HAI) 61 64; Rafael Arevalo-Gonzalez/Jaime Cuellar (ESA) d. Joel Allen/Gael Gaetjens (HAI) 63 62.

16 June Cuba defeated Haiti 3-0: Edgar Hernandez-Perez (CUB) d. Jean Marc Bazanne (HAI) 61 63; Ricardo Chile-Fonte (CUB) d. Gael Gaetjens (HAI) 63 60; Edgar Hernandez-Perez/Sandor Martinez-Breijo (CUB) d. Joel Allen/Gael Gaetjens (HAI) 64 64.

Costa Rica defeated El Salvador 2-1: Geoffrey Barton (CRC) d. Andres Weisskopf (ESA) 63 64; Federico Camacho (CRC) d. Jose Baires (ESA) 46 63 97; Rafael Arevalo-Gonzalez/Jaime Cuellar (ESA) d. Juan-Antonio Marin/Fernando Martinez-Manrique (CRC) 76(6) 64.

Play-offs for 1st-4th Positions:

Results carried forward: **Bahamas defeated Puerto Rico 3-0; El Salvador defeated Cuba 2-1.**

17 June El Salvador defeated Bahamas 3-0: Jaime Cuellar (ESA) d. Marvin Rolle (BAH) 61 64; Rafael Arevalo-Gonzalez (ESA) d. Devin Mullings (BAH) 61 64; Rafael Arevalo-Gonzalez/Jaime Cuellar (ESA) d. Devin Mullings/Marvin Rolle (BAH) 75 26 61.

Cuba defeated Puerto Rico 2-1: Gilberto Alvarez (PUR) d. Edgar Hernandez-Perez (CUB) 75 61; Ricardo Chile-Fonte (CUB) d. Jorge Rangel (PUR) 62 64; Ricardo Chile-Fonte/Sandor Martinez-Breijo (CUB) d. Gilberto Alvarez/Gabriel Montilla (PUR) 62 64.

18 June Cuba defeated Bahamas 3-0: Edgar Hernandez-Perez (CUB) d. Marvin Rolle (BAH) 75 36 63; Ricardo Chile-Fonte (CUB) d. Devin Mullings (BAH) 62 62; Favel-Antonio Freyre-Perdomo/Sandor Martinez-Breijo (CUB) d. Devin Mullings/Marvin Rolle (BAH) 61 75.

El Salvador defeated Puerto Rico 2-1: Ricardo Gonzalez-Diaz (PUR) d. Jose Baires (ESA) 63 75; Rafael Arevalo-Gonzalez (ESA) d. Jorge Rangel (PUR) 61 62; Rafael Arevalo-Gonzalez/Jaime Cuellar (ESA) d. Gilberto Alvarez/Ricardo Gonzalez-Diaz (PUR) 64 36 86.

Play-offs for 5th-8th Positions:

Results carried forward: **Trinidad & Tobago defeated Honduras 3-0; Haiti defeated Costa Rica 2-1.**

17 June Haiti defeated Trinidad & Tobago 2-1: Gael Gaetjens (HAI) d. Michael Clarke (TRI) 64 61; Shane Stone (TRI) d. Joel Allen (HAI) 64 75; Joel Allen/Jean Marc Bazanne (HAI) d. Shane Stone/Troy Stone (TRI) 62 63.

Costa Rica defeated Honduras 2-1: Jose Moncada (HON) d. Fernando Martinez-Manrique (CRC) 63 36 63; Juan-Antonio Marin (CRC) d. Calton Alvarez (HON) 61 61; Federico Camacho/Juan-Antonio Marin (CRC) d. Carlos Caceres/Jose Moncada (HON) 62 64.

18 June Costa Rica defeated Trinidad & Tobago 2-1: Federico Camacho (CRC) d. Shane Stone (TRI) 76(1) 60; Juan-Antonio Marin (CRC) d. Richard Brown (TRI) 62 62; Shane Stone/Troy Stone (TRI) d. Geoffrey Barton/Fernando Martinez-Manrique (CRC) 64 64.

Honduras defeated Haiti 3-0: Jose Moncada (HON) d. Nicolas Etienne (HAI) 61 60; Calton Alvarez (HON) d. Jean Marc Bazanne (HAI) 61 62; Calton Alvarez/Franklin Garcia (HON) d. Jean Marc Bazanne/Nicolas Etienne (HAI) 61 64.

Final Positions: 1. El Salvador, 2. Cuba, 3. Bahamas, 4. Puerto Rico, 5. Haiti, 6. Costa Rica, 7. Trinidad & Tobago, 8. Honduras.

Cuba and El Salvador promoted to Americas Zone Group II in 2007. Honduras and Trinidad & Tobago relegated to Americas Zone Group IV in 2007.

Asia/Oceania Zone

Date: 19-23 July **Venue:** Manila, Philippines **Surface:** Clay (I)
Group A: Philippines, Singapore, Sri Lanka, Vietnam
Group B: Bahrain, Bangladesh, Iran, Saudi Arabia

Group A

19 July Philippines defeated Sri Lanka 3-0: Eric Taino (PHI) d. Amrit Rupasinghe (SRI) 60 61; Cecil Mamiit (PHI) d. Harshana Godamanna (SRI) 64 62; Eric Taino/Cecil Mamiit (PHI) d. Rohan De Silva/Rajeev Rajapakse (SRI) 62 61.

Vietnam defeated Singapore 2-1: Quoc-Khanh Le (VIE) d. Stanley Armando (SIN) 62 61; Minh-Quan Do (VIE) d. Min Wee (SIN) 60 64; Heryanta Dewandaka/Kok-Huen Kam (SIN) d. Quang-Tri Lam/Thanh-Hoang Tran (VIE) 76(4) 62.

20 July Philippines defeated Singapore 3-0: Eric Taino (PHI) d. Min Wee (SIN) 60 60; Cecil Mamiit (PHI) d. Kok-Huen Kam (SIN) 61 60; Johnny Arcilla/Patrick-John Tierro (PHI) d. Kok-Huen Kam/Min Wee (SIN) 63 61.

Sri Lanka defeated Vietnam 2-1: Quoc-Khanh Le (VIE) d. Amrit Rupasinghe (SRI) 62 62; Harshana Godamanna (SRI) d. Minh-Quan Do (VIE) 62 61; Rohan De Silva/Harshana Godamanna (SRI) d. Minh-Quan Do/Quoc-Khanh Le (VIE) 64 67(4) 61.

21 July Philippines defeated Vietnam 3-0: Eric Taino (PHI) d. Thanh-Hoang Tran (VIE) 60 61; Cecil Mamiit (PHI) d. Minh-Quan Do (VIE) 75 57 61; Johnny Arcilla/Patrick-John Tierro (PHI) d. Quang-Tri Lam/Thanh-Hoang Tran (VIE) 63 75.

Sri Lanka defeated Singapore 3-0: Amrit Rupasinghe (SRI) d. Stanley Armando (SIN) 64 60; Harshana Godamanna (SRI) d. Min Wee (SIN) 61 63; Rohan De Silva/Rajeev Rajapakse (SRI) d. Kok-Huen Kam/Min Wee (SIN) 75 64.

Group B

19 July Iran defeated Saudi Arabia 3-0: Anoosha Shahgholi (IRI) d. Fahad Al Saad (KSA) 06 61 61; Ashkan Shokoofi (IRI) d. Omar Al Thagib (KSA) 61 62; Anoosha Shahgholi/Ashkan Shokoofi (IRI) d. Badar El Megayel/Fahad Al Saad (KSA) 61 64.

Bahrain defeated Bangladesh 2-1: Shibu Lal (BAN) d. Abdul-Rahman Shehab (BRN) 63 76(6); Khaled Al Thawadi (BRN) d. Sree-Amol Roy (BAN) 64 76(6); Khaled Al Thawadi/Abdul-Rahman Shehab (BRN) d. Shibu Lal/Prithul Mondal (BAN) 61 64.

20 July Iran defeated Bangladesh 3-0: Anoosha Shahgholi (IRI) d. Prithul Mondal (BAN) 63 61; Ashkan Shokoofi (IRI) d. Shibu Lal (BAN) 61 61; Ashkan Shokoofi/Farshad Talavar (IRI) d. Md Tajmul Islam/Shibu Lal (BAN) 61 64.

Saudi Arabia defeated Bahrain 2-1: Fahad Al Saad (KSA) d. Abdul-Rahman Shehab (BRN) 61 62; Khaled Al Thawadi (BRN) d. Omar Al Thagib (KSA) 60 63; Badar Al Megayel/Fahad Al Saad (KSA) d. Khaled Al Thawadi/Abdul-Rahman Shehab (BRN) 62 75.

21 July Iran defeated Bahrain 3-0: Anoosha Shahgholi (IRI) d. Khaled Al Thawadi (BRN) 64 61; Ashkan Shokoofi (IRI) d. Hamad Al Nusuf (BRN) 64 62; Mohammed Mohazebnia/Farshad Talavar (IRI) d. Khaled Al Thawadi/Abdul-Rahman Shehab (BRN) 26 64 86.

Saudi Arabia defeated Bangladesh 2-1: Fahad Al Saad (KSA) d. Prithul Mondal (BAN) 61 62; Shibu Lal (BAN) d. Omar Al Thagib (KSA) 76(6) 41 ret; Badar Al Megayel/Fahad Al Saad (KSA) d. Shibu Lal/Sree-Amol Roy (BAN) 26 63 62.

Play-offs for 1st-4th Positions:

Results carried forward: **Philippines defeated Sri Lanka 3-0; Iran defeated Saudi Arabia 3-0.**

22 July Philippines defeated Saudi Arabia 3-0: Eric Taino (PHI) d. Fahad Al Saad (KSA) 16 60 63; Cecil Mamiit (PHI) d. Saleh Al Raajeh (KSA) 60 60; Johnny Arcilla/Patrick-John Tierro (PHI) d. Badar Al Megayel/Saleh Al Raajeh (KSA) 62 62.

Iran defeated Sri Lanka 2-1: Anoosha Shahgholi (IRI) d. Amrit Rupasinghe (SRI) 61 63; Harshana Godamanna (SRI) d. Ashkan Shokoofi (IRI) 46 64 63; Anoosha Shahgholi/Ashkan Shokoofi (IRI) d. Rohan De Silva/Harshana Godamanna (SRI) 64 62.

23 July Philippines defeated Iran 3-0: Eric Taino (PHI) d. Farshad Talavar (IRI) 61 76(4); Cecil Mamiit (PHI) d. Anoosha Shahgholi (IRI) 63 61; Johnny Arcilla/Patrick-John Tierro (PHI) d. Anoosha Shahgholi/Ashkan Shokoofi (IRI) 63 61.

Sri Lanka defeated Saudi Arabia 2-1: Fahad Al Saad (KSA) d. Rajeev Rajapakse (SRI) 63 61; Harshana Godamanna (SRI) d. Saleh Al Raajeh (KSA) 64 62; Rohan De Silva/Harshana Godamanna (SRI) d. Badar Al Megayel/Fahad Al Saad (KSA) 62 60.

Play-offs for 5th-8th Positions:

Results carried forward: **Vietnam defeated Singapore 2-1; Bahrain defeated Bangladesh 2-1.**

22 July Vietnam defeated Bangladesh 2-1: Shibu Lal (BAN) d. Quoc-Khanh Le (VIE) 60 ret; Minh-Quan Do (VIE) d. Sree-Amol Roy (BAN) 64 62; Minh-Quan Do/Thanh-Hoang Tran (VIE) d. Shibu Lal/Sree-Amol Roy (BAN) 60 61.

Singapore defeated Bahrain 2-1: Abdul-Rahman Shehab (BRN) d. Heryanta Dewandaka (SIN) 64 62; Kok-Huen Kam (SIN) d. Khaled Al Thawadi (BRN) 46 75 63; Stanley Armando/Heryanta Dewandaka (SIN) d. Khaled Al Thawadi/Abdul-Rahman Shehab (BRN) 64 46 86.

23 July Vietnam defeated Bahrain 3-0: Thanh-Hoang Tran (VIE) d. Abdul-Rahman Shehab (BRN) 63 62; Minh-Quan Do (VIE) d. Hamad Al Nusuf (BRN) 60 61; Minh-Quan Do/Thanh-Hoang Tran (VIE) d. Hamad Al Nusuf/Khaled Al Thawadi (BRN) 62 63.

Singapore defeated Bangladesh 2-1: Shibu Lal (BAN) d. Min Wee (SIN) 36 63 64; Kok-Huen Kam (SIN) d. Sree-Amol Roy (BAN) 64 75; Heryanta Dewandaka/Kok-Huen Kam (SIN) d. Shibu Lal/Sree-Amol Roy (BAN) 60 62.

Final Positions: 1. Philippines, 2. Iran, 3. Sri Lanka, 4. Saudi Arabia, 5. Vietnam, 6. Singapore, 7. Bahrain, 8. Bangladesh.

Iran and Philippines promoted to Asia/Oceania Zone Group II in 2007. Bahrain and Bangladesh relegated to Asia/Oceania Zone Group IV in 2007.

Europe/Africa Zone – Venue I

Date: 19-23 July **Venue:** Banja Luka, Bosnia/Herzegovina **Surface:** Clay (O)
Group A: Andorra, Armenia, Estonia, Lithuania
Group B: Bosnia/Herzegovina, Moldova, Monaco, Turkey

Group A

19 July Lithuania defeated Andorra 3-0: Daniel Lencina-Ribes (LTU) d. Jean-Baptiste Poux-Gautier (AND) 76(5) 75; Gvidas Sabeckis (LTU) d. Paul Gerbaud-Farras (AND) 61 75; Daniel Lencina Ribes/Gvidas Sabeckis (LTU) d. Hector Hormigo/Axel Rabanal (AND) 61 60.

Estonia defeated Armenia 2-1: Jaak Poldma (EST) d. Hayk Zohranyan (ARM) 76(7) 62; Vladimir Ivanov (EST) d. Sargis Sargsian (ARM) 64 64; Sargis Sargsian/Harutyun Sofyan (ARM) d. Mikk Irdoja/Jurgen Zopp (EST) 36 61 64.

20 July Estonia defeated Lithuania 2-1: Jaak Poldma (EST) d. Daniel Lencina-Ribes (LTU) 75 60; Gvidas Sabeckis (LTU) d. Vladimir Ivanov (EST) 63 64; Jaak Poldma/Jurgen Zopp (EST) d. Daniel Lencina-Ribes/Gvidas Sabeckis (LTU) 61 63.

Armenia defeated Andorra 2-1: Jean-Baptiste Poux-Gautier (AND) d. Hayk Zohranyan (ARM) 60 61; Sargis Sargsian (ARM) d. Paul Gerbaud-Farras (AND) 64 62; Sargis Sargsian/Harutyun Sofyan (ARM) d. Paul Gerbaud-Farras/Jean-Baptiste Poux-Gautier (AND) 75 64.

21 July Lithuania defeated Armenia 2-1: Daniel Lencina-Ribes (LTU) d. Harutyun Sofyan (ARM) 62 62; Gvidas Sabeckis (LTU) d. Sargis Sargsian (ARM) 76(1) 57 63; Hayk Avetisyan/Hayk Zohranyan (ARM) d. Mindaugas Celedinas/Denis Riabuchin (LTU) 67(6) 60 62.

Estonia defeated Andorra 3-0: Mikk Irdoja (EST) d. Hector Hormigo (AND) 63 61; Jurgen Zopp (EST) d. Paul Gerbaud-Farras (AND) 63 63; Mikk Irdoja/Jaak Poldma (EST) d. Jean-Baptiste Poux-Gautier/Axel Rabanal (AND) 62 64.

Group B

19 July Monaco defeated Turkey 3-0: Guillaume Couillard (MON) d. Haluk Akkoyun (TUR) 36 63 62; Benjamin Balleret (MON) d. Ergun Zorlu (TUR) 63 61; Thomas Drouet/Emmanuel Heussner (MON) d. Baris Erguden/Alaatin-Bora Gerceker (TUR) 64 46 64.

Bosnia/Herzegovina defeated Moldova 2-1: Bojan Vujic (BIH) d. Andrei Ciumac (MDA) 63 57 61; Roman Borvanov (MDA) d. Ivan Dodig (BIH) 64 46 97; Ivan Dodig/Bojan Vujic (BIH) d. Roman Borvanov/Evghenii Plugariov (MDA) 46 60 62.

20 July Turkey defeated Moldova 3-0: Haluk Akkoyun (TUR) d. Roman Tudoreanu (MDA) 63 61; Ergun Zorlu (TUR) d. Evghenii Plugariov (MDA) 64 63; Haluk Akkoyun/Ergun Zorlu (TUR) d. Andrei Ciumac/Roman Tudoreanu (MDA) 62 62.

Monaco defeated Bosnia/Herzegovina 3-0: Guillaume Couillard (MON) d. Bojan Vujic (BIH) 75 63; Benjamin Balleret (MON) d. Aleksandar Maric (BIH) 61 63; Thomas Drouet/Emmanuel Heussner (MON) d. Ivan Dodig/Sinisa Markovic (BIH) 63 75.

21 July Turkey defeated Bosnia/Herzegovina 2-1: Haluk Akkoyun (TUR) d. Aleksandar Maric (BIH) 64 64; Ivan Dodig (BIH) d. Ergun Zorlu (TUR) 62 26 75; Haluk Akkoyun/Ergun Zorlu (TUR) d. Ivan Dodig/Bojan Vujic (BIH) 67(7) 76(9) 64.

Monaco defeated Moldova 2-1: Andrei Ciumac (MDA) d. Thomas Drouet (MON) 76(8) 62; Benjamin Balleret (MON) d. Roman Borvanov (MDA) 64 63; Guillaume Couillard/Emmanuel Heussner (MON) d. Roman Borvanov/Andrei Ciumac (MDA) 63 64.

Play-offs for 1st-4th Positions:

Results carried forward: **Estonia defeated Lithuania 2-1; Monaco defeated Turney 3-0.**

22 July Lithuania defeated Turkey 2-1: Daniel Lencina-Ribes (LTU) d. Haluk Akkoyun (TUR) 76(1) 62; Gvidas Sabeckis (LTU) d. Ergun Zorlu (TUR) 75 61; Baris Erguden/Alaatin-Bora Gerceker (TUR) d. Daniel Lencina-Ribes/Gvidas Sabeckis (LTU) 75 63.

Monaco defeated Estonia 2-1: Guillaume Couillard (MON) d. Jaak Poldma (EST) 62 46 62; Benjamin Balleret (MON) d. Jurgen Zopp (EST) 61 61; Mikk Irdoja/Jurgen Zopp (EST) d. Thomas Drouet/Emmanuel Heussner (MON) 75 ret.

23 July Monaco defeated Lithuania 3-0: Guillaume Couillard (MON) d. Daniel Lencina-Ribes (LTU) 60 62; Benjamin Balleret (MON) d. Gvidas Sabeckis (LTU) 63 63; Benjamin Balleret/Emmanuel Heussner (MON) d. Mindaugas Celedinas/Denis Riabuchin (LTU) 63 62.

Turkey defeated Estonia 2-1: Jaak Poldma (EST) d. Baris Erguden (TUR) 63 63; Ergun Zorlu (TUR) d. Vladimir Ivanov (EST) 63 64; Baris Erguden/Ergun Zorlu (TUR) d. Mikk Irdoja/Jurgen Zopp (EST) 62 46 64.

Play-offs for 5th-8th Positions:

Results carried forward: **Armenia defeated Andorra 2-1; Boznia/Herzegovina defeated Moldova 2-1.**

22 July Moldova defeated Andorra 3-0: Andrei Ciumac (MDA) d. Jean-Baptiste Poux-Gautier (AND) 64 26 63; Roman Borvanov (MDA) d. Paul Gerbaud-Farras (AND) 63 61; Roman Borvanov/Evghenii Plugariov (MDA) d. Hector Hormigo/Axel Rabanal (AND) 61 64.

Bosnia/Herzegovina defeated Armenia 3-0: Bojan Vujic (BIH) d. Hayk Zohranyan (ARM) 63 20 ret; Ivan Dodig (BIH) d. Sargis Sargsian (ARM) 64 76(4); Aleksandar Maric/Sinisa Markovic (BIH) d. Vahe Avetisyan/Harutyun Sofyan (ARM) 61 36 62.

23 July Bosnia/Herzegovina defeated Andorra 2-1: Sinisa Markovic (BIH) d. Hector Hormigo (AND) 60 60; Jean-Baptiste Poux-Gautier (AND) d. Aleksandar Maric (BIH) 76(7) 62; Ivan Dodig/Bojan Vujic (BIH) d. Paul Gerbaud-Farras/Jean-Baptiste Poux-Gautier (AND) 67(6) 76(6) 64.

Moldova defeated Armenia 3-0: Andrei Ciumac (MDA) d. Harutyun Sofyan (ARM) 61 64; Roman Borvanov (MDA) d. Hayk Zohranyan (ARM) 60 60; Andrei Ciumac/Roman Tudorcanu (MDA) d. Harutyun Sofyan/Hayk Zohranyan (ARM) 31 ret.

Final Positions: 1. Monaco, 2. Estonia, 3. Turkey, 4. Lithuania, 5. Bosnia/Herzegovina, 6. Moldova, 7. Armenia, 8. Andorra.

Estonia and Monaco promoted to Europe/Africa Zone Group II in 2007. Andorra and Armenia relegated to Europe/Africa Zone Group IV in 2007.

Europe/Africa Zone – Venue II

Date: 26-30 July **Venue:** Gaborone, Botswana **Surface:** Hard (O)
Group A: Denmark, Namibia, Rwanda, Tunisia
Group B: Botswana, Cote D'Ivoire, Ghana, Nigeria

Group A

26 July Denmark defeated Rwanda 3-0: Rasmus Norby (DEN) d. Eric Hagenimana (RWA) 62 61; Frederik Nielsen (DEN) d. Jean-Claude Gasigwa (RWA) 60 60; Jacob Melskens/Martin Pedersen (DEN) d. Alain Hakizimana/Jean-Paul Nshimiyimana (RWA) 60 60.

Namibia defeated Tunisia 2-1: Haithem Abid (TUN) d. Johan Theron (NAM) 62 63; Jurgens Strydom (NAM) d. Malek Jaziri (TUN) 62 62; Henrico Du Plessis/Jurgens Strydom (NAM) d. Haithem Abid/Hakim Rezgui (TUN) 46 76(2) 64.

27 July Denmark defeated Namibia 3-0: Rasmus Norby (DEN) d. Johan Theron (NAM) 60 61; Frederik Nielsen (DEN) d. Jurgens Strydom (NAM) 76(4) 60; Frederik Nielsen/Rasmus Norby (DEN) d. Henrico Du Plessis/Hermann Kuschke (NAM) 62 30 ret.

Tunisia defeated Rwanda 3-0: Hakim Rezgui (TUN) d. Eric Hagenimana (RWA) 60 76(4); Haithem Abid (TUN) d. Jean-Claude Gasigwa (RWA) 62 62; Haithem Abid/Wael Kilani (TUN) d. Alain Hakizimana/Jean-Paul Nshimiyimana (RWA) 61 60.

28 July Denmark defeated Tunisia 3-0: Rasmus Norby (DEN) d. Hakim Rezgui (TUN) 64 64; Frederik Nielsen (DEN) d. Haithem Abid (TUN) 63 64; Jacob Melskens/Martin Pedersen (DEN) d. Wael Kilani/Hakim Rezgui (TUN) 63 63.

Namibia defeated Rwanda 3-0: Henrico Du Plessis (NAM) d. Eric Hagenimana (RWA) 62 57 64; Jurgens Strydom (NAM) d. Jean-Claude Gasigwa (RWA) 62 61; Henrico Du Plessis/Johan Theron (NAM) d. Eric Hagenimana/Alain Hakizimana (RWA) 67(5) 63 62.

Group B

26 July Cote D'Ivoire defeated Botswana 3-0: Charles Irie (CIV) d. Bokang Setshogo (BOT) 64 64; Claude N'Goran (CIV) d. Phenyo Matong (BOT) 64 61; Terence Nugent/Laury Sylvain N'Yaba (CIV) d. Onkabetse Matong/Uyapo Nleya (BOT) 62 63.

Nigeria defeated Ghana 2-1: Gunther Darkey (GHA) d. Abdul-Mumin Babalola (NGR) 64 64; Jonathan Igbinovia (NGR) d. Henry Adjei-Darko (GHA) 61 36 63; Abdul-Mumin Babalola/Jonathan Igbinovia (NGR) d. Henry Adjei-Darko/Gunther Darkey (GHA) 76(4) 61.

27 July Nigeria defeated Cote D'Ivoire 3-0: Abdul-Mumin Babalola (NGR) d. Charles Irie (CIV) 76(3) 36 60; Jonathan Igbinovia (NGR) d. Claude N'Goran (CIV) 62 64; Abdul-Mumin Babalola/Jonathan Igbinovia (NGR) d. Terence Nugent/Laury Sylvain N'Yaba (CIV) 64 64.

Ghana defeated Botswana 2-1: Bokang Setshogo (BOT) d. Gunther Darkey (GHA) 50 def; Salifu Mohammed (GHA) d. Phenyo Matong (BOT) 67(4) 60 61; Henry Adjei-Darko/Gunther Darkey (GHA) d. Phenyo Matong/Bokang Setshogo (BOT) 60 60.

28 July Ghana defeated Cote D'Ivoire 3-0: Gunther Darkey (GHA) d. Terence Nugent (CIV) 61 62; Henry Adjei-Darko (GHA) d. Charles Irie (CIV) 62 64; Henry Adjei-Darko/Gunther Darkey (GHA) d. Charles Irie/Laury Sylvain N'Yaba (CIV) 46 64 75.

Nigeria defeated Botswana 3-0: Abdul-Mumin Babalola (NGR) d. Bokang Setshogo (BOT) 63 63; Jonathan Igbinovia (NGR) d. Phenyo Matong (BOT) 63 60; Sunday Maku/Lawal Shehu (NGR) d. Onkabetse Matong/Uyapo Nleya (BOT) 63 63.

Play-offs for 1st-4th Positions:

Results carried forward: **Denmark defeated Namibia 3-0; Nigeria defeated Ghana 2-1.**

29 July Denmark defeated Nigeria 2-1: Rasmus Norby (DEN) d. Abdul-Mumin Babalola (NGR) 62 62; Jonathan Igbinovia (NGR) d. Frederik Nielsen (DEN) 61 62; Frederik Nielsen/Rasmus Norby (DEN) d. Abdul-Mumin Babalola/Jonathan Igbinovia (NGR) 63 62.

Ghana defeated Namibia 3-0: Gunther Darkey (GHA) d. Henrico Du Plessis (NAM) 62 62; Henry Adjei-Darko (GHA) d. Jurgens Strydom (NAM) 63 62; Henry Adjei-Darko/Gunther Darkey (GHA) d. Henrico Du Plessis/Jurgens Strydom (NAM) 64 62.

30 July Denmark defeated Ghana 3-0: Rasmus Norby (DEN) d. Gunther Darkey (GHA) 64 64; Frederik Nielsen (DEN) d. Henry Adjei-Darko (GHA) 36 63 75; Jacob Melskens/Martin Pedersen (DEN) d. Emmanuel Mensah/Salifu Mohammed (GHA) 62 61.

Nigeria defeated Namibia 2-1: Abdul-Mumin Babalola (NGR) d. Henrico Du Plessis (NAM) 63 63; Jonathan Igbinovia (NGR) d. Jurgens Strydom (NAM) 76(5) 46 63; Henrico Du Plessis/Jurgens Strydom (NAM) d. Jonathan Igbinovia/Lawal Shehu (NGR) 64 76(2).

Play-offs for 5th-8th Positions:

Results carried forward: **Cote D'Ivoire defeated Botswana 3-0; Tunisia defeated Rwanda 3-0.**

29 July Tunisia defeated Cote D'Ivoire 2-1: Wael Kilani (TUN) d. Laury Sylvain N'Yaba (CIV) 64 62; Haithem Abid (TUN) d. Charles Irie (CIV) 64 62; Claude N'Goran/Terence Nugent (CIV) d. Haithem Abid/Hakim Rezgui (TUN) 46 62 62.

Botswana defeated Rwanda 3-0: Bokang Setshogo (BOT) d. Jean-Paul Nshimiyimana (RWA) 62 61; Phenyo Matong (BOT) d. Jean-Claude Gasigwa (RWA) 36 63 63; Phenyo Matong/Bokang Setshogo (BOT) d. Jean-Claude Gasigwa/Alain Hakizimana (RWA) 64 63.

30 July Tunisia defeated Botswana 3-0: Wael Kilani (TUN) d. Bokang Setshogo (BOT) 62 26 64; Haithem Abid (TUN) d. Phenyo Matong (BOT) 62 60; Haithem Abid/Wael Kilani (TUN) d. Phenyo Matong/Uyapo Nleya (BOT) 62 63.

Cote D'Ivoire defeated Rwanda 3-0: Charles Irie (CIV) d. Jean-Paul Nshimiyimana (RWA) 62 60; Claude N'Goran (CIV) d. Jean-Claude Gasigwa (RWA) 62 63; Terence Nugent/Laury Sylvain N'Yaba (CIV) d. Alain Hakizimana/Jean-Paul Nshimiyimana (RWA) 62 63.

Final Positions: 1. Denmark, 2. Nigeria, 3. Ghana, 4. Namibia, 5. Tunisia, 6. Cote D'Ivoire, 7. Botswana, 8. Rwanda.

Denmark and Nigeria promoted to Europe/Africa Zone Group II in 2007. Botswana and Rwanda relegated to Europe/Africa Zone Group IV in 2007.

GROUP IV

Americas Zone

Date: 14-18 June **Venue:** San Salvador, El Salvador **Surface:** Clay (O)
Nations: Barbados, Bermuda, Panama, St. Lucia, US Virgin Islands

14 June St. Lucia defeated Bermuda 3-0: Vernon Lewis (LCA) d. Jovan Whitter (BER) 62 61; Alberton Richelieu (LCA) d. Romar Douglas (BER) 61 63; Sirsean Arlain/Alberton Richelieu (LCA)

d. Romar Douglas/Jovan Whitter (BER) 63 63.

US Virgin Islands defeated Barbados 2-1: Kristopher Elien (ISV) d. Russell Moseley (BAR) 75 63; Eugene Highfield (ISV) d. Haydn Lewis (BAR) 61 64; Damien Applewhaite/Michael Date (BAR) d. Shane Dalton/Whitney McFarlane (ISV) 62 64.

15 June Panama defeated St. Lucia 2-1: Vernon Lewis (LCA) d. Arnulfo Courtney (PAN) 36 76(4) 86; Alberto Gonzalez (PAN) d. Alberton Richelieu (LCA) 61 36 61; Arnulfo Courtney/Alberto Gonzalez (PAN) d. Sirsean Arlain/Alberton Richelieu (LCA) 64 61.

Barbados defeated Bermuda 3-0: Russell Moseley (BAR) d. Jovan Whitter (BER) 60 63; Haydn Lewis (BAR) d. Romar Douglas (BER) 61 63; Damien Applewhaite/Michael Date (BAR) d. Romar Douglas/Tony Thompson (BER) 61 62.

16 June Panama defeated Bermuda 3-0: Arnulfo Courtney (PAN) d. David Thomas (BER) 64 60; Alberto Gonzalez (PAN) d. Romar Douglas (BER) 60 63; Alberto Gonzalez/Juan Miguel Gonzalez (PAN) d. David Thomas/Jovan Whitter (BER) 75 62.

St. Lucia defeated US Virgin Islands 3-0: Vernon Lewis (LCA) d. Kristopher Elien (ISV) 60 61; Alberton Richelieu (LCA) d. Eugene Highfield (ISV) 64 57 62; Vernon Lewis/Alberton Richelieu (LCA) d. Shane Dalton/Kristopher Elien (ISV) 63 64.

17 June Panama defeated US Virgin Islands 2-1: Arnulfo Courtney (PAN) d. Kristopher Elien (ISV) 64 60; Alberto Gonzalez (PAN) d. Eugene Highfield (ISV) 63 46 62; Kristopher Elien/Whitney McFarlane (ISV) d. Juan Miguel Gonzalez/Mario Cal (PAN) 75 63.

Barbados defeated St. Lucia 2-1: Vernon Lewis (LCA) d. Russell Moseley (BAR) 61 62; Haydn Lewis (BAR) d. Alberton Richelieu (LCA) 63 61; Haydn Lewis/Russell Moseley (BAR) d. Vernon Lewis/Alberton Richelieu (LCA) 76(4) 62.

18 June Barbados defeated Panama 2-1: Arnulfo Courtney (PAN) d. Russell Moseley (BAR) 36 60 61; Haydn Lewis (BAR) d. Alberto Gonzalez (PAN) 36 75 63; Haydn Lewis/Russell Moseley (BAR) d. Arnulfo Courtney/Alberto Gonzalez (PAN) 62 62.

US Virgin Islands defeated Bermuda 3-0: Kristopher Elien (ISV) d. Jovan Whitter (BER) 64 60; Eugene Highfield (ISV) d. David Thomas (BER) 60 61; Kristopher Elien/Eugene Highfield (ISV) d. Romar Douglas/David Thomas (BER) 61 61.

Final Positions: 1. Barbados, 2. Panama, 3. St. Lucia, 4. US Virgin Islands, 5. Bermuda.

Barbados and Panama promoted to Americas Zone Group III in 2007.

Asia/Oceania Zone

Date: 5-9 April **Venue:** Amman, Jordan **Surface:** Hard (O)
Group A: Iraq, Myanmar, Oman, Qatar
Group B: Jordan, Syria, Tajikistan, Turkmenistan, United Arab Emirates

Group A

6 April Iraq defeated Qatar 2-1: Haidar Kadhim (IRQ) d. Abdullah Hajji (QAT) 64 64; Sultan Khalfan (QAT) d. Nasir Al Hatam (IRQ) 64 62; Nasir Al Hatam/Haidar Kadhim (IRQ) d. Abdullah Hajji/Sultan Khalfan (QAT) 61 61.

7 April Oman defeated Iraq 3-0: Mohammed Al Nabhani (OMA) d. Saddam-Hussain Kadhim (IRQ) 64 62; Khalid Al Nabhani (OMA) d. Nasir Al Hatam (IRQ) 62 60; Khalid Al Nabhani/Mohammed Al Nabhani (OMA) d. Nasir Al Hatam/Akram Al Karem (IRQ) 61 62.

Oman defeated Myanmar 3-0: Mohammed Al Nabhani (OMA) d. Kyaw Zaw Naing (MYA) 61 62; Khalid Al Nabhani (OMA) d. Mg-Tu Maw (MYA) 64 63; Khalid Al Nabhani/Mohammed Al Nabhani (OMA) d. Mg-Tu Maw/Kyaw Zaw Naing (MYA) 76(4) 46 62.

Myanmar defeated Qatar 2-1: Kyaw Zaw Naing (MYA) d. Abdullah Hajji (QAT) 64 64; Sultan Khalfan (QAT) d. Mg-Tu Maw (MYA) 60 60; Mg-Tu Maw/Kyaw Zaw Naing (MYA) d. Abdullah Hajji/Sultan Khalfan (QAT) 76(6) 62.

9 April Iraq defeated Myanmar 2-1: Saddam-Hussain Kadhim (MYA) 36 61 60; Mg-Tu Maw (MYA) d. Nasir Al Hatam (IRQ) 62 64; Nasir Al Hatam/Haidar Kadhim (IRQ) d. Mg-Tu Maw/Kyaw Zaw Naing (MYA) 46 42 def.

Oman defeated Qatar 3-0: Mohammed Al Nabhani (OMA) d. Feras Al-Naama (QAT) 60 61; Khalid Al Nabhani (OMA) d. Abdullah Hajji (QAT) 61 61; Fahad-Qamar Al Hashmi/Khalid Al Nabhani (OMA) d. Feras Al-Naama/Faisal Al Jarboey (QAT) 61 62.

Final Positions: 1. Oman, 2. Iraq, 3. Myanmar, 4. Qatar.

Group B

6 April Tajikistan defeated Turkmenistan 3-0: Mirkhusein Yakhyaev (TJK) d. Dovran Chagylov (TKM) 75 63; Dilshod Sharifi (TJK) d. Ruslan Almazov (TKM) 60 61; Farhod Saidov/Dilshod Sharifi (TJK) d. Dovran Chagylov/Shirali Javliev (TKM) 61 62.

Syria defeated Turkmenistan 3-0: Issam Taweel (SYR) d. Eziz Davletov (TKM) 60 61; Hayan Maarouf (SYR) d. Shirali Javliev (TKM) 63 63; Magdi Salim/Yashar Sheet (SYR) d. Ruslan Almazov/Eziz Davletov (TKM) 61 62.

United Arab Emirates defeated Jordan 3-0: Mahmoud-Nader Al Balushi (UAE) d. Tareq Talal-Shakwa (JOR) 62 16 62; Omar Bahrouzyan-Awadhy (UAE) d. Abdullah Fadda (JOR) 63 61; Omar Bahrouzyan-Awadhy/Hamad-Abbas Ismail (UAE) d. Ahmed Al Hadid/Ahmed Tbayshat (JOR) 61 61.

7 April Tajikistan defeated Jordan 2-1: Mirkhusein Yakhyaev (TJK) d. Tareq Talal-Shakwa (JOR) 36 63 97; Dilshod Sharifi (TJK) d. Abdullah Fadda (JOR) 76(5) 36 64; Ahmed Al Hadid/Ahmed Tbayshat (JOR) d. Rahmatullo Rajabaliev/Mirkhusein Yakhyaev (TJK) 75 64.

Jordan defeated Turkmenistan 3-0: Tareq Talal-Shakwa (JOR) d. Dovran Chagylov (TKM) 60 62; Abdullah Fadda (JOR) d. Ruslan Almazov (TKM) 61 62; Abdullah Fadda/Tareq Talal-Shakwa (JOR) d. Ruslan Almazov/Dovran Chagylov (TKM) 60 64.

United Arab Emirates defeated Syria 2-1: Issam Taweel (SYR) d. Mahmoud-Nader Al Balushi (UAE) 67(6) 60 60; Omar Bahrouzyan-Awadhy (UAE) d. Hayan Maarouf (SYR) 60 61; Mahmoud-Nader Al Balushi/Omar Bahrouzyan-Awadhy (UAE) d. Magdi Salim/Issam Taweel (SYR) 62 61.

8 April Syria defeated Tajikistan 2-1: Mirkhusein Yakhyaev (TJK) d. Issam Taweel (SYR) 63 62; Hayan Maarouf (SYR) d. Dilshod Sharifi (TJK) 76(3) 16 62; Magdi Salim/Yashar Sheet (SYR) d. Dilshod Sharifi/Mirkhusein Yakhyaev (TJK) 64 64.

United Arab Emirates defeated Turkmenistan 3-0: Mahmoud-Nader Al Balushi (UAE) d. Eziz Davletov (TKM) 61 61; Omar Bahrouzyan-Awadhy (UAE) d. Ruslan Almazov (TKM) 60 60; Faisal Bastaki/Hamad-Abbas Ismail (UAE) d. Ruslan Almazov/Dovran Chagylov (TKM) 63 63.

9 April United Arab Emirates defeated Tajikistan 3-0: Mahmoud-Nader Al Balushi (UAE) d. Mirkhusein Yakhyaev (TJK) 57 63 64; Omar Bahrouzyan-Awadhy (UAE) d. Dilshod Sharifi (TJK) 67(4) 62 62; Faisal Bastaki/Hamad-Abbas Ismail (UAE) d. Rahmatullo Rajabaliev/Farhod Saidov (TJK) 62 61.

Syria defeated Jordan 2-1: Issam Taweel (SYR) d. Tareq Talal-Shakwa (JOR) 62 67(6) 62; Abdullah Fadda (JOR) d. Hayan Maarouf (SYR) 63 62; Magdi Salim/Yashar Sheet (SYR) d. Abdullah Fadda/Tareq Talal-Shakwa (JOR) 62 26 62.

Final Positions: 1. United Arab Emirates, 2. Syria, 3. Tajikistan, 4. Jordan, 5. Turkmenistan.

Oman and United Arab Emirates promoted to Asia/Oceania Zone Group III in 2007.

Europe/Africa Zone

Date: 19-23 July **Venue:** Marsa, Malta **Surface:** Hard (O)
Group A: Iceland, Malta, San Marino, Uganda
Group B: Azerbaijan, Madagascar, Mauritius

Group A

19 July Iceland defeated San Marino 2-1: Domenico Vicini (SMR) d. Andri Jonsson (ISL) 61 75; Arnar Sigurdsson (ISL) d. Diego Zonzini (SMR) 64 62; Andri Jonsson/Arnar Sigurdsson (ISL) d. Christian Rosti/Domenico Vicini (SMR) 26 61 62.

Malta defeated Uganda 2-1: Matthew Asciak (MLT) d. Patrick Olobo (UGA) 61 75; Patrick Ochan (UGA) d. Daniel Ceross (MLT) 63 76(4); Gordon Asciak/Daniel Ceross (MLT) d. Patrick Ochan/Patrick Olobo (UGA) 67(6) 75 63.

20 July Iceland defeated Malta 2-1: Matthew Asciak (MLT) d. Andri Jonsson (ISL) 60 62; Arnar Sigurdsson (ISL) d. Daniel Ceross (MLT) 62 61; Andri Jonsson/Arnar Sigurdsson (ISL) d. Gordon Asciak/Matthew Asciak (MLT) 64 76(3).

San Marino defeated Uganda 2-1: Domenico Vicini (SMR) d. Patrick Olobo (UGA) 76(4) 62; Patrick Ochan (UGA) d. Diego Zonzini (SMR) 62 62; Christian Rosti/Domenico Vicini (SMR) d. Cedric Babu/Patrick Ochan (UGA) 62 76(5).

21 July Iceland defeated Uganda 2-1: Godfrey Uzunga (UGA) d. Andri Jonsson (ISL) 67(3) 60 62; Arnar Sigurdsson (ISL) d. Patrick Ochan (UGA) 61 60; Jon Jonsson/Arnar Sigurdsson (ISL) d. Cedric Babu/Patrick Olobo (UGA) 62 62.

San Marino defeated Malta 2-1: Matthew Asciak (MLT) d. Christian Rosti (SMR) 61 64; Domenico Vicini (SMR) d. Daniel Ceross (MLT) 64 57 62; Christian Rosti/Domenico Vicini (SMR) d. Matthew Asciak/Daniel Ceross (MLT) 75 46 61.

Group B

19 July Madagascar defeated Azerbaijan 3-0: Thierry Rajaobelina (MAD) d. Farid Shirinov (AZE) 60 62; Jacob Rasolondrazana (MAD) d. Emin Agaev (AZE) 62 64; Antso Rakotondramanga/Vatsy Rakotondramanga (MAD) d. Emin Agaev/Fakhraddin Shirinov (AZE) 64 26 64.

20 July Mauritius defeated Madagascar 2-1: Thierry Rajaobelina (MAD) d. Kamil Patel (MRI) 57 60 61; Bruno Goroyam (MRI) d. Jacob Rasolondrazana (MAD) 63 46 64; Bruno Goroyam/Kamil Patel (MRI) d. Thierry Rajaobelina/Antso Rakotondramanga (MAD) 76(4) 62.

21 July Mauritius defeated Azerbaijan 2-1: Kamil Patel (MRI) d. Fakhraddin Shirinov (AZE) 60 67(6) 75; Bruno Goroyam (MRI) d. Emin Agaev (AZE) 76(1) 76(6); Emin Agaev/Ramin Hajiyev (AZE) d. Alexandre Daruty/Bruno Goroyam (MRI) 63 64.

Play-offs for 1st-4th Positions:
Results carried forward: **Iceland defeated San Marino 2-1; Mauritius defeated Madagascar 2-1.**

22 July Madagascar defeated Iceland 2-1: Thierry Rajaobelina (MAD) d. Andri Jonsson (ISL) 60 61; Arnar Sigurdsson (ISL) d. Jacob Rasolondrazana (MAD) 62 61; Thierry Rajaobelina/Jacob Rasolondrazana (MAD) d. Magnus Gunnarsson/Jon Jonsson (ISL) 62 60.

Mauritius defeated San Marino 2-1: Kamil Patel (MRI) d. Diego Zonzini (SMR) 61 61; William Forcellini (SMR) d. Alexandre Daruty (MRI) 63 16 62; Bruno Goroyam/Kamil Patel (MRI) d. Christian Rosti/Domenico Vicini (SMR) 75 26 63.

23 July Mauritius defeated Iceland 3-0: Kamil Patel (MRI) d. Magnus Gunnarsson (ISL) 60 60; Bruno Goroyam (MRI) d. Jon Jonsson (ISL) 61 62; Bruno Goroyam/Kamil Patel (MRI) d. Magnus Gunnarsson/Jon Jonsson (ISL) 61 61.

Madagascar defeated San Marino 3-0: Thierry Rajaobelina (MAD) d. Diego Zonzini (SMR) 62 63; Antso Rakotondramanga (MAD) d. William Forcellini (SMR) 60 64; Vatsy Rakotondramanga/Jacob Rasolondrazana (MAD) d. Domenico Vicini/Diego Zonzini (SMR) 63 63.

Play-offs for 5th-7th Positions:
Results carried forward: **Malta defeated Uganda 2-1.**

22 July Malta defeated Azerbaijan 2-1: Phillip Zarb Mizzi (MLT) d. Ramin Hajiyev (AZE) 75 61; Fakhraddin Shirinov (AZE) d. Daniel Ceross (MLT) 36 61 ret; Gordon Asciak/Matthew Asciak (MLT) d. Emin Agaev/Fakhraddin Shirinov (AZE) 60 61.

23 July Azerbaijan defeated Uganda 3-0: w/o.

Final Positions: 1. Mauritius, 2. Madagascar, 3. Iceland, 4. San Marino, 5. Malta, 6. Azerbaijan, 7. Uganda.

Iceland, Madagascar, Mauritius and San Marino promoted to Europe/Africa Zone Group III in 2007.

ACKNOWLEDGMENTS

SITTING HALFWAY UP THE STAND at the Olympic Stadium in Moscow, commentating radio-style on the final for Daviscup.com, it suddenly hit me just how global the Davis Cup is. That may seem a fatuous remark from someone who has been covering Davis Cup ties since 1988, but it was the surge of emails and other electronic messages we received from listeners right around the globe that did it. Many of them were expatriate Russians, many more were expatriate Argentinians, but a fair few were just fans of tennis who were reveling in the excitement and the spectacle, the angst and the anguish of a truly gripping piece of theatre. My own family is scattered across the globe, but at that moment I understood the full meaning of the term "tennis family"—my co-commentators, Craig Gabriel and Eli Weinstein, and I were the intermediaries communicating to people across the whole world, and as we received emails from listeners, we ticked off the continents they'd written from to prove it.

To everyone who contacted us during our commentary on the Davis Cup Final, a huge thank you. You have helped shape the spirit in which I have tried to reflect the Davis Cup by BNP Paribas in 2006. There are also a host of other people who were my eyes and ears at all the ties I couldn't attend. In alphabetical order they are: Nicola Arzani, Alfredo Bernardi, Tim Curry, Stephen Duckitt, Diana Gabanyi, Craig Gabriel, Gordan Gabrovec, Chris Guccione, Sandy Harwitt, Marcel Hauck, Pedro Hernandez, Dieter Koditek, Alberto Mancini, Marcella Mesker, Marco Mordasini, Leo Schlink, Gregor Sket, Rene Stauffer, Dmitry Tursunov, and Rodrigo Valdebenito.

I could not have got to so many ties without the invaluable and far-sighted support of Barbara Travers and her team in the ITF Communications department. Special thanks go to Andrew Rigby, for whom 2006 was his last Davis Cup year, and the editor of this book who started the year as Joanne Sirman and finished it as Joanne Burnham, showing that there is time between Davis Cup weekends for getting married.

Finally, more thanks than I can ever convey to the long-suffering Louise and Tamara, the two most important people in my life who I miss very much when I'm away from home. Tamara turned five and started school in the week of the Davis Cup semifinals, by which time I had bought her an inflatable globe so she could see where her dad gets to. If she ends up being good at geography, she too can thank the Davis Cup.

Chris Bowers

PHOTOGRAPHY CREDITS

- Ron Angle: 32, 33, 34, 44 (top right), 48/49, 57, 58, 59, 60, 64 (top left), 65 (bottom right and bottom middle), 67, 100 (bottom left), 116 (top right upper)
- Siggi Bucher: 26, 27, 28, 29, 44 (top left), 47, 89, 90, 91, 101 (top right), 103
- Sergio Carmona: 30, 31, 44 (bottom left), 65 (top right), 80 (top right), 84/85, 92 (except top), 93, 100 (top left), 117 (bottom left)
- Antoine Couvercelle: 61, 62, 63, 65 (bottom left)
- Jeff Crow: 44 (bottom right), 54, 55, 56, 64 (bottom left), 65 (top left), 81 (bottom right)
- GEPA: 38, 39, 40, 81 (top left), 98, 100 (bottom right), 101 (top left lower)
- Robert Ghement: 97, 101 (bottom right)
- Manuel Gonzalez: 35, 36, 37, 64 (top middle)
- Henk Koster: 22, 23, 24, 25, 96, 116 (bottom left)
- Sergio Llamera: 14/15, 41, 42, 43, 45 (top right), 64 (top middle lower and bottom right), 75, 76, 77, 78, 79, 80 (bottom left), 116 (top left and top right lower), 117 (top left and top right)
- Laci Perenyi: 86, 87, 88
- Photonews: 64 (top right), 80 (bottom right), 94, 95
- Marcelo Ruschel: 45 (top left and bottom left upper), 81 (top right lower), 99, 100 (top right)
- Paul Zimmer: 16, 17, 18, 19, 20, 21, 45 (bottom right), 50, 51, 52, 53, 68/69, 70, 71, 72, 73, 74, 80 (top left), 81 (top right and bottom left), 83, 101 (top left)
- Paul Zimmer/Andrei Golovanov: cover (front and back), endpapers (front and back), 6, 8, 11, 12, 104/105, 106, 107, 108, 109, 110, 111, 112, 113, 114, 115, 116 (bottom right), 117 (bottom right), 119